Richard C. Nicholson's translation of R
is an exposition of the 'nature and con
light of the doctrines of Vedānta which echoes the Upanishadic
'there is one only without a second.' Other traditional views like Nyāya, Vaisesika, Sānkhya, Yoga and Mīmāmsā are referred to wherever necessary. The book opens with a broad outline of Vedānta and then passes on to a through discussion of other relevant topics such as, *Prakriti* and *Purusha*, *ātmā* (personality), *buddhi* (intellect), *manas* (mind), *kosha* (wraps), *sūkshma* (subtle) and *sthūla* (gross) forms, stages of the *ātman* like alertness, dream and slumber and finally concludes with three essays on *moksha* (final release).

All those interested in Hindu philosophy shall find this book instructive and absorbing; for nowhere else shall they find this abstract subject treated in so compact, yet clear, manner.

Man and His Becoming

Man and His Becoming
according to the Vedānta

René Guénon

translated by
Richard C. Nicholson

Munshiram Manoharlal
Publishers Pvt. Ltd.

ISBN 978-81-215-0901-5 (HB)
ISBN 978-81-215-0902-2 (PB)
Indian edition 2011

PRINTED IN INDIA
Published by Vikram Jain *for*
Munshiram Manoharlal Publishers Pvt. Ltd.
PO Box 5715, 54 Rani Jhansi Road, New Delhi 110 055, INDIA

www.mrmlbooks.com

Contents

Preface

On several occasions, in previous writings, we have expressed the intention of undertaking a series of studies that would aim, according to the needs of the case, either at presenting a direct exposition of various aspects of the Eastern metaphysical doctrines or at making such adaptations of them as might seem most intelligible and advantageous, while however always remaining strictly faithful to their spirit. The present work constitutes the first of these studies. For reasons which have already been explained elsewhere, we have taken the Hindu doctrines as our central authority, and more especially the teaching of the Vedānta, which is the most purely metaphysical branch of these doctrines. It should however be clearly understood that there is nothing in this procedure to prevent us, as occasion arises, from pointing out analogies and making comparisons with other theories, regardless of their origin; in particular we shall refer to the teachings of other orthodox branches of the Hindu doctrine insofar as they clarify or complete the teachings of the Vedānta on various points. To anyone inclined to raise objections to the adoption of such a method we would reply that such criticism is all the less justifiable in that our intentions are in no wise those of a historian; we wish to re-assert emphatically, at this point, that our purpose is not erudition but understanding, and that it is the truth of ideas which interests us exclusively. If therefore it has seemed desirable in the present instance to supply precise references, we have done so for reasons quite unconnected with the special preoccupations of orientalists; we simply wished to show that we have invented nothing and that the ideas expounded derive from a genuine traditional source; at the same time, for the sake of those who are able to profit thereby, we have furnished the means of referring to texts containing complementary information, for it goes without saying that we make no claim to put forward an absolutely complete exposition of the doctrine, even regarding a single point.

As for an exposition of the entire doctrine, such a thing would be a sheer impossibility; either it would involve an interminable labour, or it would require to be put in so synthetic a form as to be quite incomprehensible to Western readers. Moreover, in a work of that sort, it would be extremely difficult to avoid an appearance of systematisation which is incompatible with the most essential characteristics of the metaphysical doctrines; doubtless this would amount to no more than an appearance, but none the less it would inevitably be productive of extremely serious errors, all the more so since Western people, by reason of their mental habits, are only too prone to discover "systems" even where none exist. One must for ever be on one's guard against affording the slightest pretext for unjustifiable assimilations of this kind; better abstain altogether from expounding a doctrine than contribute towards denaturing it, even if merely through clumsiness. Fortunately, however, there is a way out of the difficulty; this consists in treating a particular point or one more or less definite aspect of the doctrine at a time, leaving oneself free to take up other points afterwards, in order to make them in their turn the subject of other separate studies. Moreover there will never be any danger of these studies becoming what the erudite and the specialists call "monographs", because the fundamental principles will never be lost sight of, and the secondary points themselves can therefore only appear as direct or indirect applications of those principles, from which all else derives; in the metaphysical order, that is to say in the realm of the Universal, there can be no place at all for "specialisation".

From the foregoing remarks it should be clear why we have restricted the scope of the present study to the nature and constitution of the human being: to make our comments intelligible we shall naturally be obliged to touch upon other subjects which at first sight may appear to be beside the point, but it will always be in relation to this one subject that we shall introduce them. The principles themselves are possessed of a range vastly exceeding the entire field of their possible applications; but it is none the less legitimate to expound them, wherever such a thing is possible, in relation to this or that particular application, and this is a procedure which in fact offers considerable advantages. Moreover, it is only insofar as any question, no matter what, is related to principles that it can be said to be treated metaphysically; it is this truth which must never be lost sight of, so long as it is intended to treat of genuine metaphysic and not of the pseudo-metaphysic of European philosophers.

If we have embarked first upon the exposition of questions relative to the human being, that is not because these questions enjoy any exceptional importance in themselves from the purely metaphysical point of view: that point of view being essentially detached from every contingency, the case of man can never appear to it as a privileged one. We have begun with the discussion of these questions simply because they have already been raised during the course of our previous writings and thus a complementary work such as the present one now seems called for. The order in which any subsequent studies may appear will depend similarly on circumstances and will largely be determined by considerations of expediency; we think it advisable to mention this at the outset lest anyone should be tempted to see some sort of hierarchical order in our works, either as regards the importance of the questions treated or as regards their interdependence one upon another: that would be to attribute to us an intention which we have never entertained, but we know only too well how easily such misunderstandings arise, and that is why we take steps to forestall them whenever it lies within our power to do so.

There is a further point which is of too great importance to be passed over without comment in these preliminary observations, although we thought we have explained ourselves sufficiently clearly on other occasions; but we have noticed that some people have failed to grasp our meaning and it is therefore advisable to emphasize it still further. Genuine knowledge, which alone concerns us, has little if anything at all to do with "profane" knowledge; the studies which go to make up the latter cannot be looked upon even as an indirect path of approach to "Sacred Science"; on the contrary, at times they even constitute an obstacle, by reason of the often irremediable mental deformation which is the commonest consequence of a certain kind of education. For the understanding of doctrines such as those we are expounding a study undertaken merely "from the outside" is of no avail; as we have already remarked, it is not a question of history or philology or literature; and we will add, at the risk of repeating ourselves to a degree which some may consider fastidious, it is not a question of philosophy either. All these things, indeed, belong to that order of knowledge which we class as "profane" or "external", not from contempt, but because it is in fact nothing else; one is not called upon to consider whom one may happen to please or displease; one simply has to describe things as they are, giving to each thing the name and rank which normally belong to it. The fact that in the modern West "Sacred Science" has been odiously caricatured by more or less conscious imposters is not a reason for keeping silent about it, or for ignoring, if not actually repudiating it; on the contrary, we declare unhesitatingly not only that it exists, but also that it is our sole preoccupation. Anyone who cares to refer to what we have already said elsewhere about the extravagances of the occultists and theosophists will not fail to understand that we are alluding here to something of quite a different order and that the attitude of people of that kind also can never be regarded by us as anything but "profane" : moreover they only make their case worse by pretending to a knowledge which is not theirs, and this is one of the principal reasons why we find it necessary to expose the absurdity of their pretended doctrines whenever the occasion presents itself.

From the preceding remarks it should also be clear that the doctrines we propose to discuss refuse to lend themselves, owing to their very nature, to any attempt at "popularisation"; it would be foolish to try "to bring within everybody's reach"—to use a common phrase of our time—conceptions which can only come within the grasp of an elect, and to attempt to do so would be the surest way of distorting them. We have explained elsewhere what we mean by the intellectual elect, and what part it will be called upon to play if it ever comes to be formed in the West; while at the same time we have shown how a genuine and profound study of the Eastern doctrines is indispensable in preparing for its formation. It is in view of this work, the results of which no doubt will only make themselves felt after a long interval, that we believe it necessary to expound certain ideas for the benefit of those who are capable of assimilating them, without however modifying or simplifying them after the fashion of the "popularisers," which would be in flat contradiction with our avowed intentions. Indeed, it is not for the doctrine to abase and reduce itself to the level of the limited understanding of the many; it is for those who are capable of it to raise themselves to the understanding of the doctrine in its integral purity, and it is only in this way that a genuine intellectual elect can be formed. Among several persons who receive an identical teaching, each one understands and assimilates it more or less completely and profoundly according to the range of his own intellectual possibilities, and in this way selection, without which there could be no genuine hierarchy, comes about quite naturally. These questions have already been dealt with previously, but it was necessary to recall them before embarking upon a strictly doctrinal exposition; and the more unfamiliar they are to Western minds today, the more imperative it is to emphasize them.

Chapter 1

General Remarks on the Vedānta

The Vedānta, contrary to an opinion widely held among orientalists, is neither a philosophy nor a religion, nor does it partake to a greater or lesser extent of the character of either. Deliberately to consider this doctrine under these aspects is one of the gravest of errors, calculated to result in failure to understand anything about it from the outset; in fact, one reveals oneself thereby as a complete stranger to the true character of Eastern thought, the modes of which are quite different from those of the West and do not permit of inclusion within the same categories. We have already explained in a previous work that religion, if one is not to extend the scope of this word beyond its just limits, is something wholly Western; the same term cannot be applied to Eastern doctrines without stretching its meaning to such a degree that it becomes quite impossible to give it any definition, even of the vaguest kind. As for philosophy, it also represents an exclusively Western point of view, one, moreover, much more external than the religious point of view and therefore still further removed from that of the subject we are about to study. As we said above, it is an essentially "profane"[1] kind of knowledge even when it is not purely illusory, and we cannot help thinking, particularly when we consider what philosophy has become in modern times, that its absence from a civilization is hardly a matter for regret. In a recent book a certain orientalist has asserted that "philosophy is philosophy everywhere," a statement which opens the door to undesirable assimilations of every kind, including those against which he himself quite justly protected on other occasions. That philosophy is to be found everywhere is just what we are at present contesting; and we decline to accept as "universal thought" (to adopt a phrase of the same author) what is in reality but an extremely special mode of thought. Another historian of the Eastern doctrines, while in principle admitting the inadequacy and inexactitude of those Western terms which have been persistently imposed upon them, nevertheless declared that he could see no way of dispensing with such terms, and he made as free a use of them as any of his predecessors. This appears all the more surprising inasmuch as for our part we have never experienced the slightest need to resort to this philosophical terminology, which would still suffer from the disadvantage of being somewhat repellent and needlessly complicated, even if it were not wrongly applied, as is always the case under such circumstances. But we do not wish to embark at present upon the kind of discussions to which these questions might give rise; we were merely concerned with showing, by these examples, how difficult it is for some people to step outside the "classical" framework within which their Western education has confined their thought from the outset.

To return to the Vedānta, it must be regarded in reality as a purely metaphysical doctrine, opening up truly unlimited possibilities of conception, and, as such, it can in no wise be contained within the more or less narrow framework of any system whatsoever. In this respect and without looking any further, one can observe a profound and irreducible difference, a difference of principle, distinguishing it from anything that Europeans include under the name of philosophy. Indeed the avowed aim of all philosophical conceptions, especially among the moderns, who carry to extremes the individualist tendency and the resultant quest for originality at any price, is precisely to establish systems that are complete and definite, or in other words essentially relative and limited on all sides. Fundamentally a system is nothing but a closed conception, the more or less narrow limits of which are naturally determined by the "mental horizon" of its author. But all systematization is absolutely impossible in pure metaphysic, where everything belonging to the individual order is truly non-existence, metaphysic being entirely detached from all relativities and contingencies, philosophical or otherwise. This is necessarily so, because metaphysic is essentially knowledge of the Universal, and such knowledge does not permit of being enclosed within any formula, however comprehensive.

The diverse metaphysical and cosmological conceptions of India are not, strictly speaking, different doctrines, but only developments of a single doctrine according to different points of view and in various, but by no means in compatible, directions. Besides, the Sanskrit word *darshana,* which is attached to each of these conceptions, properly signifies "view" or "point of view", for the verbal root *drish,* whence it is derived, has as its primary meaning that of "seeing": it cannot in any way denote, "system", and if orientalists translate it thus, that is merely the result of Western habits of thought which lead them into false assimilations at every step. Seeing nothing but philosophy everywhere, it is only natural that they should also see systems wherever they go.

The single doctrine to which we have just alluded is represented essentially by the Veda, that is to say, the sacred and traditional Science in its integrality, for this precisely is the proper meaning of that term.[2] It furnishes the principle and the common basis of all the more or less secondary and derivative branches which go to make up those diverse conceptions in which certain people have seen so many rival and opposed systems. In reality, these conceptions, insofar as they are in accord with their principle, obviously cannot contradict one another; on the contrary, they are bound mutually to complete and elucidate each other. Moreover, there is no need to read into this statement the suggestion of a more or less artificial and belated "syncretism" for the entire doctrine must be considered as being synthetically comprised within the Veda, and that from its origin. Tradition, in its integrality, forms a perfectly coherent whole, which however does not mean to say a systematic whole; and since all the points of view which it comprises can as well be considered simultaneously as in succession, there cannot be any real object in enquiring into the historical order in which they may actually have been developed and rendered explicit, even apart from the fact that the existence of oral transmission, probably lasting over a period of indefinite duration, would render any proposed solution quite misleading. Though the exposition may be modified to a certain degree externally in order to adapt itself to the circumstances of this or that period, it is none the less true that the basis of tradition always remains exactly the same, and that these external modifications in no wise reach or affect the essence of the doctrine.

The concordance of a conception with the fundamental principle of the tradition is the necessary and sufficient condition of its orthodoxy, which term must however on no account be taken in this instance merely according to its religious mode; it is necessary to stress this point in order to avoid any error in interpretation, because in the West there is generally no question of orthodoxy except as viewed from the purely religious standpoint. In everything that concerns metaphysic or that proceeds more or less directly from it, the heterodoxy of a conception is fundamentally not different from its falsity, resulting from its disagreement with the essential principles. Since these are contained in the Veda, it follows that it is agreement with the Veda that constitutes the criterion of orthodoxy. Heterodoxy is found, therefore, at that point where contradiction with the Veda arises; whether voluntary or involuntary, it indicates a more or less far-reaching deviation or alteration of the doctrine, which moreover generally occurs only within somewhat restricted schools and can only affect special points, sometimes of very secondary importance, the more so since the power inherent in the tradition has the effect of limiting the scope and bearing of individual errors, of eliminating those which exceed certain hounds, and in any case, of preventing them from becoming widespread and acquiring real authority. Even where a partially heterodox school has become to a certain extent representative of a *darshana,* such as the Atomist school in the case of the Vaisheshika, no slur is cast on the legitimacy of that *darshana* in itself; for it to remain within the bounds of orthodoxy it is only necessary to reduce it again to its truly essential content. On this point we cannot do better than quote by way of general indication this passage from the *Sānkhya Pravachana-bhāshya* of Vijnāna Bhikshu: "In the doctrine of Kanāda (the Vaisheshika) and in the Sānkhya (of Kapila), the portion which is contrary to the Veda must be rejected by those who adhere strictly to the orthodox tradition; in the doctrine of Jaimini and that of Vyāsa (the two Mīmānsās), there is nothing which is not in accordance with the Scriptures (considered as the basis of that tradition)."

The name Mīmānsā, derived from the verbal root *man,* "to think," in its iterative form, denotes the reflective study of the "Sacred Science": it is the intellectual fruit of meditation on the Veda. The first Mīmānsā (Pūrva-mīmānsā) is attributed to Jaimini; but we must recall in this connection that the names which are thus attached to the formulation of the different *darshanas* cannot be related in any way to particular individuals: they are used symbolically to describe what are really "intellectual aggregates," composed of all those who have devoted themselves to one and the same study over the course of a period the duration of which is no less indeterminable than the date of its beginning. The first Mīmānsā is also called "Karma-mīmānsā" or practical Mīmānsā because it is concerned with actions, and more particularly, with the accomplishment of rites. The word *karma* indeed possesses a double meaning: in a general sense, it means action in all its forms; in a special and technical sense, it means ritual action, such as is prescribed by the Veda. This practical Mīmānsā has for its aim, as the commentator Somanātha says, "to determine in an exact and precise manner the sense of the Scriptures", but chiefly insofar as they include precepts, and not in respect of pure knowledge or *jnāna,* which is often placed in opposition to *karma,* an opposition corresponding precisely to the distinction between the two Mīmānsās.

The second Mīmānsā (Uttara-mīmānsā) is attributed to Vyāsa, that is to say to the "collective entity" which arranged and finally codified the traditional texts constituting the Veda itself. This attribution is particularly significant, for it is easy to see that it is not a historical or legendary person with whom we are dealing in this instance, but a genuine "intellectual function", amounting one may say, to a permanent function, since Vyāsa is described as one of the seven *chirajīvis,* literally "beings endowed with longevity," whose existence is not confined to any particular epoch.[3] To describe the second Mīmānsā in relation to the first, one may regard it as belonging to the purely intellectual and contemplative order. We cannot say theoretical Mīmānsā, by way of symmetry with practical Mīmānsā, because this description would give rise to ambiguity. Although the word "theory" is indeed etymologically synonymous with contemplation, it is none the less true that in current speech it has come to convey a far more restricted meaning; in a doctrine which is complete from the metaphysical point of view, theory, understood in this ordinary sense, is not self-sufficient, but is always accompanied or followed by a corresponding "realization," of which it is, in short, but the indispensable basis, and in view of which it is ordained, as the means in view of the end.

The second Mīmānsā is further entitled Brahma-mīmānsā, as being essentially and directly concerned with "Divine Knowledge" (*Brahma-vidyā*). It is this which constitutes the Vedānta strictly speaking, that is to say, according to the etymological significance of that term, the "end of the Veda," based principally upon the teaching contained in the Upanishads. This expression "end of the Veda" should be understood in the double sense of conclusion and of aim. On the one hands, the Upanishads do in fact form the last portion of the Vedic texts, and, on the other hand, that which is taught therein, in so far at least as it can be taught, is the final and supreme aim of traditional knowledge in its entirety, detached from all the more or less particular and contingent applications derivable from it. In other words, with the Vedānta, we find ourselves in the domain of pure metaphysic.

The Upanishads, forming an integral part of the Veda, are one of the very foundations of the orthodox tradition, a fact which has not prevented certain orientalists, such as Max Müller, from professing to detect in them the germs of a Buddhism interpreted after the modern fashion, that is to say of heterodoxy; such a statement obviously amounts to a contradiction in terms, and it would assuredly be difficult to carry misunderstanding further. One cannot insist too strongly on the fact that it is the Upanishads which here represent the primordial and fundamental tradition and consequently constitute the Vedānta in its essence; it follows from this that in a case of doubt as to the interpretation of the doctrine, it is always to the authority of the Upanishads that it is necessary to appeal in the last resort.

The principal teachings of the Vedānta, as extracted expressly from the Upanishads, have been co-ordinated and synthetically formulated in a collection of aphorisms known either as the *Brahma-sūtras* or the Shārīraka-mīmānsā;[4] the author of these aphorisms, who is called Bādarāyana and Krishna-Dwaipāyana, is identified with Vyāsa. It is important to note that the *Brahma-sūtras* belong to the class of traditional writings called Smriti, while the Upanishads, like all the other Vedic texts, form part of Shruti; but the authority of Smriti is derived from that of Shruti on which it is based. Shruti is not "revelation" in the religious and Western sense of the word, as most orientalists would have it, who, here again, confuse two very different points of view, it is the fruit of direct inspiration, so that it is in its own right that it holds its authority. "Shruti," says Shankarāchārya, "is a means of direct perception (in the sphere of transcendent knowledge), since, in order to be an authority it is necessarily independent of all other authority; while Smriti plays a part analogous to that of induction, in that it derives its authority from an authority other than itself."[5] But to avoid any misunderstanding as to the force of the analogy thus indicated between transcendent and sensory knowledge, it is necessary to add that, like every true analogy, it must be applied inversely;[6] thus, while induction rises above sensible perception and permits one to pass on to a higher level, it is on the contrary direct perception or inspiration alone which, in the transcendent order, attains to the Principle itself, to what is highest, after which nothing remains but to draw the consequences and to determine the manifold applications. It may further be said that the distinction between Shruti and Smriti is, fundamentally, equivalent to that between immediate intellectual intuition and reflective consciousness; if the first is described by a word bearing the primitive meaning of "hearing," this is precisely in order to indicate its intuitive character, and because sound holds, according to the Hindu cosmological doctrine, the primordial rank among sensible qualities. As for Smriti, its primitive meaning is "memory": in fact, memory, being but a reflex of perception, can be taken as denoting, by extension, everything which possesses the character of reflective or discursive, that is to say, of indirect knowledge. Moreover, if knowledge is symbolized by light, as is most often the case, pure intelligence and recollection, otherwise the intuitive faculty and the discursive faculty, can be respectively represented by the sun and the moon. This symbolism, which we cannot enlarge upon here, is capable of numerous applications.[7]

The *Brahma-sūtras*, the text of which is extremely concise, have given rise to numerous commentaries, the most important of which are those by Shankarāchārya and Rāmānuja; they are, both of them, strictly orthodox, so that we must not exaggerate the importance of their apparent divergencies, which are in reality more in the nature of differences of adaptation. It is true that each school is naturally enough inclined to think and to maintain that its own point of view is the most worthy of attention and ought, while not excluding other views, nevertheless to take precedence over them. But in order to settle the question in all impartiality one has but to examine these points of view in themselves and to ascertain how far the horizon extends which they embrace respectively; it is, moreover, self-evident that no school can claim to represent the doctrine in a total and exclusive manner. It is nevertheless quite certain that Shankarāchārya's point of view goes deeper and further than that of Rāmānuja; one can, moreover, infer this from the fact that the first is of Shivaite tendency while the second is clearly Vishnuite. A curious argument has been raised by M. Thibaut, who translated the two commentaries into English: he suggests that that of Rāmānuja is more faithful to the teaching of the *Brahma-sūtras* but at the same time recognises that that of Shankarāchārya is more in conformity with the spirit of the Upanishads. In order to be able to entertain such an opinion it is obviously necessary to maintain that there exist doctrinal differences between the Upanishads and the *Brahma-sūtras;* but even were this actually the case, it is the authority of the Upanishads which must prevail, as we have explained above, and Shankarāchārya's superiority would thereby be established, although this was probably not the intention of M. Thibaut, for whom the question of the intrinsic truth of the ideas concerned hardly seems to arise. As a matter of fact, the *Brahma-sūtras,* being based directly and exclusively on the Upanishads, can in no way be divergent from them; only their brevity, rendering them a trifle obscure when they are isolated from any commentary, might provide some excuse for those who maintain that they find in them something besides an authoritative and competent interpretation of the traditional doctrine. Thus the argument is really pointless, and all that we need retain is the observation that Shankarāchārya has deduced and developed more completely the essential contents of the Upanishads: his authority can only be questioned by those who are ignorant of the true spirit of the orthodox Hindu tradition, and whose opinion is consequently valueless. In a general way, therefore, it is his commentary that we shall follow in preference to all others.

To complete these preliminary observations we must again make it clear, although we have already explained this elsewhere, that it is incorrect to apply the denomination of "Esoteric Brāhmanism" to the teachings of the Upanishads, as some persons have done. The inadmissibility of this expression arises especially from the fact that the word "esoterism" is a comparative, and that its use necessarily implies the correlative existence of an "exoterism"; but such a division cannot be applied to the doctrine in question. Exoterism and esoterism, regarded not as two distinct and more or less opposed doctrines, which would be quite an erroneous view, but as the two aspects of one and the same doctrine, existed in certain schools of Greek antiquity; there is also a clear example of this relationship to be met with in the Islamic tradition, but the same does not apply in the case of the more purely Eastern doctrines. In their case one can only speak of a kind of "natural esoterism," such as inevitably pertains to every doctrine, especially in the metaphysical sphere, where it is important always to take into account the inexpressible, which is indeed what matters most of all, since words and symbols, all told, serve no purpose beyond acting as aids to conceiving it, by supplying "supports" for a task which must necessarily remain a strictly personal one. From this point of view, the distinction between exoterism and esoterism would amount to no more than the distinction between the "letter" and the "spirit"; and one could also apply it to the plurality of meanings of greater or lesser depth contained in the traditional texts, or if preferred, the sacred scriptures of all races. On the other hand it goes without saying that the same teaching is not understood in an equal degree by all who receive it: among such persons there are therefore those who in a certain sense discern the esoterism, while others, whose intellectual horizon is narrower, are limited to the exoterism; but it is not in this way that people who talk about "Esoteric Brāhmanism" understand that expression: As a matter of fact, in Brāhmanism, the teaching is accessible in its entirety to all those who are intellectually "qualified" (*adhikārī*), that is, capable of deriving a real advantage from it; and if there are doctrines reserved for a chosen few, it is because it cannot be otherwise where instruction is apportioned with discretion and in accordance with the real capacities of men. Although the traditional teaching is not esoteric in the strict sense of the word, it is indeed "initiatory," and it differs profoundly in all its methods from that "profane" education which the credulity of modern Westerners so strangely overrates: this we have already pointed out when speaking of "Sacred Science" and of the impossibility of "popularising" it.

This last observation prompts us to a further remark. In the East the traditional doctrines always employ oral teaching as their normal method of transmission, even in cases where they have been formulated in written texts; there are profound reasons for this, because it is not merely words that have to be conveyed, but above all it is a genuine participation in the tradition which has to be assured. In these circumstances, it is meaningless to say, with Max Müller and other orientalists, that the word Upanishad denotes knowledge acquired "by sitting at the feet of a teacher"; this title, if such were the meaning, would then apply without distinction to all parts of the Veda; moreover, it is an interpretation which has never been suggested or admitted by any competent Hindu. In reality, the name of the Upanishads denotes that they are ordained to destroy ignorance by providing the means of approach to supreme Knowledge; and if it is solely a question of approaching, then that is because the supreme Knowledge is in its essence strictly incommunicable, so that none can attain to it save by himself alone.

Another expression which seems to us even more unhappy than "Esoteric Brāhmanism" is "Brāhmanic Theosophy," which has been used by M. Oltramare; and he indeed admits that he did not adopt it without hesitation, since it seems "to justify the claims of Western theosophists" to have derived their sanction from India, claims which he perceives to be ill-founded. It is true that we must certainly avoid anything which might lend countenance to certain most undesirable confusions; but there are still graver and more decisive reasons against admitting the proposed designation. Although the self-styled theosophists of whom M. Oltramare speaks are almost completely ignorant of the Hindu doctrines, and have derived nothing from them but a terminology which they use entirely at random, they have no connection with genuine Theosophy either, not even with that of the West; and this is why we insist on distinguishing carefully between "Theosophy" and "Theosophism". But leaving Theosophism out of account, it can still be said that no Hindu doctrine, or more generally still, no Oriental doctrine, has enough points in common with Theosophy to justify describing it by that name; this follows directly from the fact that the word denotes exclusively conceptions of mystical inspiration, therefore religious and even specifically Christian ones. Theosophy is something peculiarly Western; why seek to apply this same word to doctrines for which it was never intended, and to which it is not much better suited than are the labels of the philosophical systems of the West? Once again, it is not with religion that we are dealing here, and consequently there cannot be any question of Theosophy any more than of Theology; these two terms, moreover, began by being almost synonymous, although, for purely historical reasons, they have come to assume widely differing acceptations.[8]

It will perhaps be objected that we have ourselves just made use of the phrase "Divine Knowledge," which is equivalent, after all, to the original meaning of the words "Theosophy" and "Theology". This is true, but in the first place, we cannot regard the last-named terms exclusively from an etymological standpoint, for they are among those with reference to which it has by now become quite impossible to ignore the changes of meaning which long usage has brought about. Moreover, we readily admit that this term "Divine Knowledge" is not itself entirely adequate; but owing to the unsuitability of European languages for the purpose of expression purely metaphysical ideas, there was no better expression available. Besides, we do not think that there are any serious objections to its use, since we have already been careful to warn the reader not to apply a religious shade of meaning to it, such as it must almost inevitably bear when related to Western conceptions. All the same, a certain ambiguity might still remain, for the Sanskrit term which can be least inaccurately rendered by "God" is not *Brahma,* but *Īshwara.* However, the adjective "divine", even in current speech, is used less strictly, more vaguely perhaps, and therefore lends itself better to such a transposition as we make here than the substantive whence it was derived. The point to note is that such terms as "Theology" and "Theosophy," even when regarded etymologically and apart from all intervention of the religious point of view, can only be translated into Sanskrit as *Īshwara-vidyā;* on the other hand, what we render approximately as "Divine Knowledge," when dealing with the Vedānta, is *Brahma-vidyā,* for the purely metaphysical point of view essentially implies the consideration of *Brahma* or the Supreme Principle, of which *Īshwara,* or the "Divine Personality," is merely a determination, as Principle of, and in relation to, universal Manifestation. The consideration of *Īshwara* therefore already implies a relative point of view; it is the highest of the relativities, the first of all determinations, but it is none the less true that it is "qualified" (*saguna*) and "conceived distinctively" (*savishesha*), whereas *Brahma* is "unqualified" (*nirguna*), "beyond all distinctions" (*nirvishesha*) absolutely unconditioned, universal manifestation in its entirety being strictly nil beside Its Infinity. Metaphysically, manifestation can only be considered from the point of view of its dependence upon the Supreme Principle and in the quality of a mere "support" for raising oneself to transcendent Knowledge; or again, taking things in the inverse order, as an application of the principal Truth. In any case, nothing more should be looked for in everything appertaining thereto than a kind of "illustration" ordained to facilitate the understanding of the Unmanifested, the essential object of metaphysic, thus permitting, as we explained when interpreting the title of the Upanishads, of an approach being made to knowledge unqualified.[9]

References

1. A single exception can be made for the very special sense in which the word is used in reference to the "Hermetic philosophy"; but it goes without saying that it is not this unusual sense that we at present have in mind, a sense which is moreover almost unknown to the moderns.
2. The root *vid*, from which Veda and *vidyā* are derived, bears the two-fold meaning of "seeing" (*videre* in Latin) and "knowing" (as in the Greek οιδα): sight is taken as a symbol of knowledge because it is its chief instrument within the sensible order; and this symbolism is carried even into the purely intellectual realm, where knowledge is likened to "inward vision", as is implied by the use of words such as "intuition" for example.
3. Something similar is to be found in other traditions: thus in Taoism they speak of eight "Immortals", elsewhere we have Melchisedec who is "without father, without mother, without descent, having neither beginning of days, nor end of life" (St. Paul, *Epistle, to the Hebrews* VII, 3); and it would probably be easy to discover yet other parallelisms of a similar kind..
4. The term *shārīraka* has been interpreted by Rāmānuja in his commentary (*Shrī-bhāshya*) on the *Brahma-sūtras*, Adhyāya I, Pāda I, sūtra 13, as referring to the "Supreme Self" (*Paramātmā*) which is in a sense "incorporated" (*shārīra*) in all things.
5. In Hindu logic, perception (*pratyaksha*) and induction or inference (*anumāna*) are the two "means of proof" (*pramānas*) that can be legitimately employed in the realm of sensible knowledge.
6. In the Hermetic tradition, the principle of analogy is expressed by the following sentence from the *Emerald Table*: "That which is below is like that which is above, and that which is above is like that which is below"; but in order to understand this formula and apply it correctly it is necessary to refer it to the symbol of "Solomon's Seal", made up of two superposed triangles pointing opposite ways.
7. Traces of this symbolism are to be detected even in speech: for example, it is not without reason that the same root *man* or *men* has served, in various languages, to form numerous words denoting at one and the same time the moon, memory, the "mental faculty" or discursive though and man himself insofar as he is specifically a "rational being."
8. A similar remark could be made with regard to the terms "astrology" and "astronomy," which were originally synonyms; among the Greeks either term

denoted both the meanings which these terms have later come to convey separately.

9. For a fuller account of all these preliminary questions, which have had to be treated in rather summary fashion in the present chapter, we would refer the reader to our *Introduction to the Study of the Hindu Doctrines* (English translation published by Luzac, London, 1945; reprinted, New Delhi, 1993), where these matters form the main subject of study and have been discussed in greater detail.

CHAPTER 2

Fundamental Distinction between the "Self" and the "Ego"

In order thoroughly to understand the teaching of the Vedānta as it pertains to the human being, it is essential to define from the start, as clearly as possible, the fundamental distinction between the "Self", which is the very principle of the being, and the individual "ego". It is hardly necessary to explain that the use of the term "Self" does not imply on our part any indentity of view with certain schools who may have used this word, but who, under an Oriental terminology, generally misunderstood, have never set forth any but purely Western views, highly fantastic at that; we are alluding here not only to Theosophism, but also to certain pseudo-Oriental schools which have entirely distorted the Vedānta under the pretext of adapting it to the Western mentality. The misuse which may have been made of a word does not, in our opinion, provide adequate grounds for declining to employ it, except where it is possible to replace it by another word equally well suited to express the same meaning, which is not the case in this instance; besides, too great a strictness on this score would undoubtedly leave very few terms indeed at one's disposal, especially as there exist hardly any which at one time or another have not been misapplied by some philosopher. The only words which we intend to reject are those invented deliberately to express views which have nothing in common with what we are expounding: such, for example, are the denominations of the different kinds of philosophical systems; such, also, are the terms which belong specifically to the vocabulary of the occultists and other "neo-spiritualists"; as for terms which the last-named have merely borrowed from earlier doctrines which they habitually and shamelessly plagiarize without understanding anything about them, we obviously need have no scruples about employing such words, while at the same time restoring the meaning which normally belongs to them.

In place of the terms "Self" and "ego", we may also use those of "Personality" and "individuality," with one reservation, however, for the "Self," as we shall explain later on, may denote something over and above the personality. The Theosophists, who seem to have taken a delight in confusing their terminology, interpret the Personality and the individuality in a sense which is the exact opposite of that in which they should rightly be understood; it is the first which they identify with the "ego," and the second with the "Self". Previously, on the contrary, even in the West, whenever any distinction has been made between these two terms, the Personality has always been regarded as superior to the individuality and that is why we say that this is their normal relationship, which there is every reason to retain. Scholastic philosophy, in particular, has not overlooked this distinction, but it does not seem to have grasped its full metaphysical significance, nor to have extracted the most profound consequences which follow from it; this is moreover what often occurs, even on occasions where Scholasticism shows the most remarkable similarity with certain portions of the Oriental doctrines. In any case, the Personality, metaphysically speaking, has nothing in common with what modern philosophers so often call the "human person," which is, in fact, nothing but the individuality pure and simple; besides, it is this alone and not the Personality which can strictly be called human. In a general way, it appears that Westerners, even when they attempt to carry their views further than those of the majority, mistake for the Personality what is actually but the superior part of the individuality, or a simple extension of it[1]: in these circumstances everything which is of the purely metaphysical order necessarily remains outside their comprehension.

The "Self" is the transcendent and permanent principle of which the manifested being, the human being, for example, is only a transient and contingent modification, a modification which, moreover, can in no way affect the principle, as will be explained more fully in what follows. The "Self", as such, is never individualized and cannot become so, for since it must always be considered under the aspect of the eternity and immutability which are the necessary attributes of pure Being, it is obviously not susceptible of any particularization, which would cause it to be "other than itself." Immutable in its own nature, it merely develops the indefinite possibilities which it contains within itself, by a relative passing from potency to act through an indefinite series of degrees. Its essential permanence is not thereby affected, precisely because this process is only relative, and because this development is, strictly speaking, not a development at all, except when looked at from the point of view of manifestation, outside of which there can be no question of succession, but only of perfect simultaneity, so that even what is virtual under one aspect, is found nevertheless to be realized in the "eternal present." As regards manifestation, it may be said that the "Self" develops its manifold possibilities, indefinite in their multitude, through a multiplicity of modalities of realization, amounting, for the integral being, to so many different states, of which states one alone, limited by the special conditions of existence which define it, constitutes the portion or rather the particular determination of that being which is called human individuality. The "Self" is thus the principle by which all the states of the being exist, each in its own domain; and this must be understood not only of the manifested states of which we have just been speaking, whether individual like the human state or supra-individual, but also,—although the word "exist" then becomes inappropriate,—of the unmanifested state, comprising all the possibilities which are not susceptible of any manifestation, as well as the possibilities of manifestation themselves in principal mode; but the "Self" derives its being from itself alone, and neither has nor can have, in the perfect and indivisible unity of its nature, any principle which is external to it.[2]

The "Self", considered in this manner, in relation to a being, is properly speaking the Personality; one might, it is true, restrict the use of this latter word to the "Self" as principle of the manifested states, just as the "Divine Personality," *Īshwara*, is the Principle of universal Manifestation; but one can also extend it analogically to the "Self" as principle of all the states of the being, manifested and unmanifested. The Personality is an immediate determination, primordial and non-particularized, of the principle which in Sanskrit is called *Ātmā* or *Paramātmā*, and which, in default of a better terms, we may call the "Universal Spirit," on the clear understanding, however, that in this use of the word "spirit" nothing is implied which might recall Western philosophical conceptions, and, in particular, that it is not turned into a correlative of "matter," as the modern mind is prone to do, being subject in this respect, even though unconsciously, to the influence of Cartesian dualism.[3] Genuine metaphysic, let it be repeated once more in this connection, lies quite outside all the oppositions of which that existing between "spiritualism" and "materialism" affords us the type, and it is in no way required to concern itself with the more or less special and often quite artificial questions which such oppositions give rise to.

Ātmā permeates all things, which are, as it were, its accidental modifications, and according to Rāmānuja's expression, "constitute in some sort its body (this word being taken here in a purely analogical sense), be they moreover of an intelligent or non-intelligent nature," that is, according to Western conceptions, "spiritual" as well as "material," for that distinction, implying merely a diversity of conditions in manifestation, makes no sort of difference in respect of the unconditioned and unmanifested Principle. This, in fact, is the "Supreme Self" (the literal rendering of *Paramātmā*) of all that exists, under whatever mode, and it abides ever "the same" through the indefinite multiplicity of the degrees of Existence, understood in the universal sense, as well as beyond Existence, that is, in principal non-manifestation.

The "Self", in relation to any being whatsoever, is in reality identical with *Ātmā,* since it is essentially beyond all distinction and all particularization; and that is why, in Sanskrit, the same word *ātman,* in cases other than the nominative, replaces the reflexive pronoun "itself." The "Self" is not therefore really distinct from *Ātmā,* except when one considers it particularly and "distinctively" in relation to a being, or, more accurately, in relation to a certain definite state of that being, such as the human state, and insofar as one considers it from this special and limited point of view alone. In this case, moreover, the "Self" does not really become distinct from *Ātmā* in any way, since as we said above, it cannot be "other than itself", and obviously cannot be affected by the point of view from which we regard it, any more then by any other contingency. What should be noted is that, to the extent that we make this distinction, we are departing from the direct consideration of the "Self" in order to consider its reflection in human individuality or in some other state of the being, for, needless to say, when confronted with the Self, all states of manifestation are strictly equivalent and can be regarded in the same way; but just now it is the human individuality which more particularly concerns us. The reflection in question determines what may be called the centre of this individuality; but if isolated from its principle, that is, from the "Self", it can only enjoy a purely illusory existence, for it is from that principle that it derives all its reality, and it effectually possesses this reality only through participation in the nature of the "Self", that is, insofar as it is identified therewith by universalization.

The Personality let us insist once more, belongs essentially to the order of principles in the strictest sense of the word, that is, to the universal order; it cannot therefore be considered from any point of view except that of pure metaphysic, which has precisely the Universal for its domain. The pseudo-metaphysicians of the West are in the habit of confusing with the Universal things which, in reality, pertain to the individual order; or rather, as they have no conception at all of the Universal, that to which they fallaciously apply this name is usually the general, which is properly speaking but a mere extension of the individual. Some carry the confusion still further; the "empiricist" philosophers, who cannot even conceive the general, identify it with the collective, which by right belongs to the particular order only; and by means of these successive degradations they end by reducing all things to the level of sensory knowledge, which many indeed regard as the only kind of knowledge possible, because their mental horizon does not extend beyond this domain and because they wish to impose on everybody else the limitations which are but the effect of their own incapacity, whether inborn or acquired through a particular form of education.

To obviate all misunderstandings of the kind which we have just described and in order to avoid tedious repetition, we will here, once and for all, provide the following table, which sets forth the essential distinctions in this connection, and to which we ask our readers to refer whenever necessary.

Universal	General Particular
Individual	Collective Singular

It is important to add that the distinction between the Universal and the Individual must not be regarded as a correlation, for the second of these two terms, being strictly annulled in respect of the first, cannot in any way be opposed to it. The same holds good with regard to the unmanifested and the manifested. Moreover, it might at first sight appear that the Universal and the unmanifested should coincide, and from a certain point of view their identification would in fact be justified, since, metaphysically, it is the unmanifested which is the all-essential. However, account must be taken of certain states of manifestation which, being formless, are from that very fact supra-individual; if, therefore, we only distinguish between the Universal and the Individual we shall be forced to assign these states to the Universal, which we are the better able to do inasmuch as it is a question of a manifestation which is still in a way principal, at least by comparison with individual states; but this, it should be clearly understood, must not lead us to forget that all that is manifested, even at this higher level, is necessarily conditioned, that is to say, relative. If we regard things in this manner, the Universal will no longer consist solely of the unmanifested, but will also extend to the formless, comprising both the unmanifested and the supra-individual states of manifestation. As for the individual, it includes all degrees of formal manifestation, that is, all states in which beings are invested with forms, for what properly characterizes individuality and essentially constitutes it as such is precisely the presence of form among the limitative conditions which define and determine a given state of existence. We can now sum up these further considerations in the following table:

Universal	The Unmanifested	
	Formless Manifestation	
Individual	Formal Manifestation	Subtle state
		Gross state

The terms "subtle state" and "gross state", which are assigned to the different degrees of formal manifestation, will be explained later; but we may point out now that this last distinction only holds good on condition that we take as our starting point the human individuality, or more precisely, the corporeal and sensible world. The "gross state" in fact is nothing else than corporeal existence itself, to which, as we shall see, human individuality belongs by one of its modalities only, and no in its integral development. As to the "subtle state", it includes, in the first place, the extra-corporeal modalities of the human being, or of every other being situated in the same state of existence, and also, in the second place, all other individual states. It is therefore evident that these two terms are not truly symmetrical and cannot even have any common measure, since one of them represents only a portion of one out of the indefinite multiplicity of states which constitute formal manifestation, while the other includes all the remainder of this manifestation.[4] Symmetry up to a certain point is to be found on condition that we restrict ourselves to the consideration of the human individuality alone, and it is, moreover, from this point of view that the distinction in question is in the first place established by the Hindu doctrine. Even if one afterwards transcends this point of view, or even if it has only been entertained with the ulterior object of transcending it effectively, it remains nevertheless true that it must inevitably be taken as a basis and term of comparison, since it relates to the state in which we actually find ourselves at the present moment.

It may be said, therefore, that the human being, considered in its integrality, comprises a certain sum of possibilities which constitute its corporeal or gross modality, and in addition, a multitude of other possibilities, which, extending in different directions beyond the corporeal modality, constitute its subtle modalities; but all these possibilities together represent, none the less, one and the same degree of universal Existence. It follows from this that human individuality is at once much more and much less than Westerners generally suppose it to be: much more, because they recognize in it scarcely anything except the corporeal modality, which includes but the smallest fraction of its possibilities; much less, however, because this individuality, far from really constituting the whole being, is but one state of that being among an indefinite multitude of other states. Moreover the sum of all these states is still nothing at all in relation to the Personality, which alone is the true being, because It alone represents its permanent and unconditioned state, and because there is nothing else which can be considered as absolutely real. All the rest is, no doubt, real also, but only in a relative way, by reason of its dependence upon the Principle and insofar as it reflects. It in some degree, as the image reflected in a mirror derives all its reality from the object it reflects and could enjoy no existence apart from it; but this lesser reality, which is only participative, is illusory in relation to the Supreme

Reality, as the image is also illusory in relation to the object; and if we should attempt to isolate it from the Principle, this illusion would become a pure and simple non-entity. We thus observe that existence, that is to say, conditioned and manifested being, is at once real in one sense and illusory in another; and this is one of the essential points which Western writers, who have distorted the Vedānta by their erroneous and highly prejudiced interpretations, have failed to grasp.

We must furthermore warn philosophers more especially that the Universal and the Individual are by no means for us what they call "categories"; and we will recall to mind—for the more modern among them seem to have forgotten it somewhat—that "categories" in the Aristotelian sense of the word are nothing but the most general of all genera, so that they still belong to the individual domain, of which, moreover, they denote the limit from a certain point of view. It would be more correct to compare with the Universal what the Scholastics term "transcendentals," which do precisely transcend all genera, including the "categories"; but although these "transcendentals" belong indeed to the universal order, it would still be a mistake to suppose that they constitute the whole of the Universal or even that they are the most important consideration in pure metaphysic; they are co-extensive with Being, but they do not transcend Being, at which point, moreover, the doctrine in which they are thus considered stops short. Although "ontology" does indeed pertain to metaphysic, it is very far from constituting metaphysic in its entirely, for Being is not the Unmanifest in itself, but only the principle of manifestation; consequently, that which is beyond Being itself. In other words, it is *Brahma* and not *Īshwara* which must be recognized as the Supreme Principle. This is declared expressly and above all by the *Brahma-sūtras,* which open with these words: "Now begins the study of *Brahma,*" to which Shankarāchārya adds the following commentary: "This first *sūtra,* while enjoining the quest of *Brahma,* advises a reflective study of the texts of the Upanishads carried out with the aid of a dialectic which (taking them as its basis and principle) is never in disagreement with them, and which, like them (but only in the capacity of simple auxiliary means), envisages 'Deliverance' as the goal."

References

1. M. Léon Daudet in certain of his works (*L'Hérédô* and *Le Monde des Images*) had distinguished in the human being between what he calls "self " (*soi*) and "ego" (*moi*); but both of these, as he conceives them, are for us equally included in the individuality and fall entirely within the scope of psychology which, whatever he may have supposed, is quite incapable of extending its sway so far as to include the Personality; however, the fact of having tried to establish such a distinction indicates a kind of presentiment which deserves to be pointed out as remarkable in an author who had no pretensions to be called a metaphysician.
2. It is our intention to set forth more completely in other works the metaphysical theory of the being's multiple states; here we need only touch on those aspects of that theory that are the indispensable to an understanding of the constitution of the human being.
3. In theology, when it is declared that "God is pure spirit" it is reasonable to suppose that this statement must likewise not be taken in the sense of "spirit" as opposed to "matter", that is to say, according to the sense in which these two terms have no meaning except in reference to one another; to understand it in this way would amount to accepting a king of "demiurgic" conception, more or less akin to the theories attributed to the Manichaeans. It is none the less true to say that such an expression is of a kind that readily lends itself to false interpretations, leading to the substitution of "a being" for pure Being.
4. This asymmetry can be made more intelligible by applying to it a well established observation of ordinary logic; whenever an attribution or quality of any kind is considered, all possible things are automatically divided into two groups, namely on the one hand things endowed with this quality and on the other hand things devoid of it; but, while the first-named group if found to be thus positively defined and determined, the second, which is only characterised in a wholly negative manner, is in no wise limited thereby and is in reality indefinite. Thus, there is neither symmetry nor any common measure between the two groups, which do not really constitute a twofold division, since their distinction holds good merely from the special point of view of a certain quality taken as a starting-point; the second group possesses no homogeneity and may include things having nothing in common with one another, which however, does not rob this division of its validity under the original terms of reference. Now it is precisely in this manner that the manifested can be distinguished from the unmanifested; so also, within the manifested, a similar distinction can be made between the formal and the formless and lastly, within the realm of form itself, between the corporeal and incorporeal.

CHAPTER 3

The Vital Centre of the Human Being, Seat of Brahma

The "Self", as we have seen in the previous chapter, must not be regarded as distinct from *Ātmā,* and, moreover, *Ātmā* is identical with *Brahma* Itself. This is what may be called the "Supreme Identity," according to an expression borrowed from Moslem esoterism, where the doctrine on this and on many other points in fundamentally the same as in Hindu tradition, in spite of great differences of form. The realization of this identity is brought about through *yoga,* that is to say, through the intimate and essential union of the being with the Divine Principle, or, if it is preferred, with the Universal. The exact meaning of this word *yoga* is in fact "union," neither more nor less,[1] despite the numerous interpretations, each more fanciful than the last, which orientalists and theosophists have suggested. It should be noted that this realization ought not strictly speaking to be considered as an "achievement", or as "the production of a non-pre-existing result," according to Shankarāchārya's expression, for the union in question, even though not actually realized in the sense here intended, exists none the less potentially, or rather virtually: it is simply a matter of the individual (for it is only in respect of the individual that one can speak of realization) becoming effectively conscious of what really is from all eternity.

That is why it is said that it is *Brahma* which dwells in the vital centre of the human being; this is true of every human being, not only of one who is actually "united" or "delivered"—these two words indeed denoting the same thing viewed under two different aspects, the first in relation to the Principle, the second in relation to manifested or conditioned existence. This vital centre is considered as corresponding analogically with the smaller ventricle (*guhā*) of the heart (*hridaya*); but it must not be confused with the heart in the ordinary sense of the word, that is to say with the physiological organ bearing that name, since it is in reality the centre not only of the corporeal individuality, but of the integral individuality, capable of indefinite extension in its own sphere (which occupies, moreover, but one degree of existence), and of which the corporeal modality constitutes only a portion, and indeed, as we have already stated, only a very limited portion. The heart is regarded as the centre of life, and in fact, from the physiological point of view, it is so by reason of its connection with the circulation of the blood, with which vitality itself is essentially linked in a very special way, as all traditions are unanimous in recognising; but it is further considered as a centre on a higher plane and in a more symbolical sense, through its connection with the universal Intelligence (in the sense of the Arabic term *el-Aqlu*) as related to the individual. It should be noted in this connection that the Greeks themselves, and Aristotle among others, assigned the same part to the heart, also making it the seat of intelligence, if one may so express it, and not of feeling as the moderns commonly do; the brain, in actual fact, is only the instrument of the mental faculty, that is, of thought in its reflective and discursive mode: and thus, in accordance with a symbolism which we have previously mentioned, the heart corresponds to the sun and the brain to the moon. It goes without saying, moreover, that in describing the centre of the integral individuality as the heart, the greatest care should be taken not to regard what is merely an analogy as an identification; between the two there is strictly speaking a correspondence only, in which, it may be added, there is nothing arbitrary, but which is perfectly valid, although our contemporaries no doubt may be led by their habits of thought to disregard the profound reasons for such a thing.

"In this seat of *Brahma* (*Brahma-pura*)," that is to say, in the vital centre of which we have just been speaking "there is a small lotus, a place in which is a small cavity (*dahara*) occupied by Ether (*Ākāsha*); we must seek That which is in this place, and we shall know It."[2]

That which, in fact, dwells at the centre of the individuality is not merely the ethereal element, the principle of the four other sensible elements, as might be supposed by those who confine themselves to its most external meaning, that relating to the corporeal world only. In the latter world this element does in fact play the part of a principle, but in a wholly relative sense, inasmuch as this world is eminently relative, and it is precisely this acceptation which has to be analogically transposed. It is indeed only in the capacity of a "support" for this transposition that Ether is mentioned here; the conclusion of the text expressly denotes this, since if nothing more were really being referred to, there would obviously be nothing to seek. And it may further be added that the lotus and the cavity in question must also be regarded symbolically, for such a "localization" is in no wise to be conceived literally once the point of view of corporeal individuality has been transcended, the other modalities being no longer subject to the spatial condition.

Nor is what we are at present considering merely the "living soul" (*jīvātmā*), that is to say, the particularised manifestation of the "Self" in life (*jīva*) and consequently in the human individual, viewed here more especially under the vital aspect which is one of the conditions of existence specifically determining the human individual state, and which applies moreover to the sum-total of modalities comprised in that state. Metaphysically, in fact, this manifestation should not be regarded separately from its Principle, which is the "Self"; and although this appears as *jīva* in the sphere of individual existence, in illusory mode therefore, it is *Ātmā* in its supreme Reality. "This *Ātmā,* which dwells in the heart, is smaller than a grain of rice, smaller than a grain of barley, smaller than a grain of mustard, smaller than a grain of millet, smaller than the germ which is in the grain of millet; this *Ātmā,* which dwells in the heart, is also greater than the earth (the sphere of gross manifestation), greater than the atmosphere (the sphere of subtle manifestation), greater than the sky (the sphere of formless manifestation), greater than all the worlds together (that is, beyond all manifestation, being the unconditioned)."[3] This is so, in fact, because analogy is necessarily applied in an inverse sense as we have already pointed out, and just as the image of an object is inverted relatively to that object, that which is first or greatest in the principal order, is, apparently at any rate, last and smallest in the order of manifestation.[4] To make a comparison with mathematics by way of clarification, it is thus that the geometrical point is quantitatively nil and does not occupy any space, though it is the principle by which space in its entirety is produced, since space is but the development of its intrinsic virtualities.[5] Similarly, though arithmetical unity is the smallest of numbers if one regards it as situated in the midst of their multiplicity, yet in principle it is the greatest, since it virtually contains them all and produces the whole series simply by the indefinite repetition of itself. The "Self" is only potentially in the individual so long as "Union" is not achieved,[6] and this is why it is comparable to a grain or a germ; but the individual, and manifestation in its entirety, exist through it alone and have no reality except through participation in its essence; while it immensely transcends all existence, being the sole Principle of all things.

When we say that the "Self" is potentially in the individual, and that "Union" exists only virtually before its realization, it goes without saying that this must be understood only from the point of view of the individual himself. In point of fact, the "Self" is not affected by any contingency, since it is essentially unconditioned; it is immutable in its "permanent actuality," and therefore there cannot be anything potential about it. Moreover, it is important to distinguish very carefully between "potentiality" and "possibility." The first of these two words implies aptitude for a certain development; it presupposes a possible "actualization" and can only be applied therefore in respect of "becoming" or of manifestation; possibilities, on the contrary, viewed in the principial and unmanifested state, which excludes all "becoming," can in no way be regarded as potential. To the individual, however, all possibilities which transcend him appear as potential, since so long as he regards himself in separative mode, deriving his own being seemingly from himself, whatever he attains is strictly speaking but a reflection and not those possibilities themselves: and although this is only an illusion, we may say that for the individual they always remain potential, since it is not as an individual that he can attain them, for, once they are realized, no individuality really exists any longer, as we shall explain more fully when we come to speak of "Deliverance." Here, however, we need to place ourselves outside the individual point of view, although, even while declaring it illusory, we none the less recognise in it that degree of reality which belongs to it within its own order; even when we do come to consider the individual, it can only be in virtue of his essential dependence upon the Principle, sole basis of that reality, and insofar as, virtually and effectively, he is integrated with the whole being; metaphysically, all must ultimately be related to the Principle, which is the "Self".

Thus, the dweller in the vital centre is, from the physical point of view, ether; from the psychic point of view, it is the "living soul," and thus far we have not transcended the realm of individual possibilities; but also, and from the metaphysical point of view, above all, it is the principial and unconditioned "Self". It is therefore, in the truest sense, the "Universal Spirit" (*Ātmā*), which is in reality *Brahma* Itself, the "Supreme Ruler"; and thus the description of this centre as *Brahma-pura* is found to be fully justified. But *Brahma,* considered in this manner as within man (and one might consider It in like manner in relation to every other state of the being) is called *Purusha;* because It rests or dwells in the individuality (we are dealing, let us repeat once more, with the integral individuality, and not merely with individuality restricted to its corporeal modality) as in a city (*puri-shaya*), for *pura,* in its proper and literal sense, signifies "city."[7]

In the vital centre, dwelling of *Purusha,* "the sun shines not, nor the moon, nor the stars; still less this visible fire (the igneous sensible element, or *tejas,* of which visibility is the peculiar quality). All shine by the radiance of *Purusha* (by reflecting its brightness); it is by its splendour that this whole (the integral individuality regarded as "microcosm") is illuminated".[8] So, too, we read in the *Bhagavadgītā*[9]: "One must seek the place (symbolizing a state) whence there is no return (to manifestation) and take refuge in the primordial *Purusha* from whom hath issued the original impulse (of universal manifestation).... This place neither sun, nor moon, nor fire illumines; it is there I have my supreme abode."[10] *Purusha* is represented as light (*jyotis*), because light symbolizes Knowledge: and it is the source of all other light, which is but its reflection, no relative knowledge being able to exist save by participation, however indirect or remote, in the essence of supreme Knowledge. In the light of this Knowledge all things are in perfect simultaneity, for principially, there cannot be anything but an "eternal present," since immutability excludes all succession; and it is only in the sphere of the manifested that the relations of possibilities which, in themselves, are eternally contained in the Principle, are transposed in terms of succession. "This *Purusha,* of the size of a thumb (*angushtha-mātra,* an expression which must not be taken literally as denoting a spatial dimension, but which refers to the same idea as the comparison with a grain),[11] is of a clear luminosity like a smokeless fire (without any admixture of obscurity or ignorance); it is the Lord of the past and of the future (being eternal, therefore omnipresent, in such wise that it contains in its permanent actuality all that appears as past or future relatively to any given moment of manifestation, a relationship that is, moreover, capable of transference beyond that particular mode of succession which is time proper); it is today (in the actual state which constitutes the human individuality) and it will be tomorrow (and in all cycles or states of existence) such as it is (in itself, principially, to all eternity."[12]

References

1. The root of this word is to be found, scarcely altered, in the Latin *jungere* and its derivatives: and the English word "yoke" shows this root in a form almost identical with the Sanskrit.
2. *Chhāndogya Upanishad,* Prapāthaka VIII, Khanda 1, shruti 3.
3. Ibid., Prapāthaka III, Khanda 14, shruti 3. In this context one cannot help recalling the Gospel parable: "The Kingdom of heaven is like to a grain of mustard seed, which a man took, and sowed in his field: which indeed is the least of all seed: but when it is grown, it is the greatest among herbs, and becometh a tree, so that the birds of the air come and lodge in the branches thereof." (*St. Matthew,* XIII, vv. 31 and 32). Though the point of view is certainly a different one, it is easy to understand how the conception of the "Kingdom of Heaven" can be transposed metaphysically; the growing of the tree stands for the development of possibilities; and there is no single feature of the parable even to the "birds of the air," representing in this case the higher states of the being, which does not recall a similar symbolism occurring in another text of the Upanishads: "Two birds, inseparably united companions, dwell in the same tree; the one eats of the fruit of the tree, while the other looks on without eating." (*Mundaka Upanishad,* Mundaka III, Khanda 1, shruti 1; *Shwetāshwatara Upanishad,* Adhyāya IV, shruti 6). The first of the two birds is *jīvātmā,* who is involved in the realm of action and its consequences; the second is the unconditioned *Ātmā,* which is pure Knowledge; and if they are inseparably associated, this is because the former is only distinguishable from the latter in an illusory manner.
4. The same idea is very clearly expressed in the Gospel "So the last shall be first and the first last." (*St. Matthew,* XX, 16).
5. Even from a more external point of view, that of ordinary elementary geometry, the following observation can be made: by continuous displacement the point engenders the line, the line engenders the surface, and the surface engenders the solid; but in the contrary sense, a surface is the intersection of two solids, a line is the intersection of two surfaces, a point is the intersection of two lines.

6. In reality, however, it is the individual who dwells in the "Self," and the being becomes effectively conscious of this when "Union" is realized; but this conscious realization implies a freeing from the limitations that constitute individuality as such, and which, in a more general way, condition all manifestation. When it is said of the "Self" that it is in a certain sense indwelling in the individual, this means that one has taken up the viewpoint of manifestation, and this is yet another example of application in an inverse sense.
7. This explanation of the word *Purusha* should of course not be regarded as an etymological derivation; it belongs to *Nirukta,* that is to say to the science of interpretation chiefly based on the symbolical value of the elements out of which words are built up. This method is generally not understood by orientalists; it is however fairly closely comparable to the method found in the Jewish *Quabbalah,* and it was not even entirely unknown to the Greeks, examples being found in the *Cratylus* of Plato. As for the meaning of *Purusha,* it may be pointed out that *puru* expresses the idea of "plenitude."
8. *Katha Upanishad,* Adhyāya II, Valli 6, shruti 15: *Mundaka Upanishad,* Mundaka II, Khanda 2, shruti 10; *Shwetāshwatara Upanishad,* Adhyāya VI, shruti 14.
9. It is well known that the *Bhagavadgītā* is an episode in the *Mahābhārata* and in this connection it should also be remembered that the Itihāsas, namely, the *Rāmāyana* and the *Mahābhārata,* being included in the Smriti, are therefore something quite different from mere "epic poems" in the profane sense of the expression as understood by Westerners.
10. *Bhagavadgītā,* XV, 4 and 6. In these texts one can observe an interesting similarity with the following passage from the description of the "Heavenly Jerusalem" in the *Apocalypse,* XXI, 23: "And the city had no need of the sun, neither of the moon, to shine in it: for the glory of God did lighten it, and the Lamb is the light thereof." From this it can be seen that the Heavenly Jerusalem is not unrelated to the "city of *Brahman*"; and for those who are aware of the relationship between "the Lamb" of Christian symbolism and the Vedic *Agni,* this comparison is still more significant. In order to preclude any false interpretations, it can be said, without unduly stressing the last point, that we are in no wise trying to suggest that *Agnus* and *Ignis* (the Latin equivalent of *Agni*) are related etymologically; but resemblances such as the one that connects these two words often play an important part in symbolism; and moreover, in our view, there is nothing fortuitous in this, since everything, including forms of language, has a reason for its existence. It is also worth noting, in the same context, that the vehicle of *Agni* is a ram.
11. A comparison could also be made here with the "endogeny of the Immortal," as it is taught by the Taoist tradition.
12. *Katha Upanishad,* Adhyāya II, Valli 4, shrutis 12 and 13. In the Islamic esoteric doctrine the same idea is expressed, in almost identical terms, by Mohyiddin ibn Arabi in his *Treatise on Unity* (*Risālatul-Ahadiyah*): "He (*Allah*) is now such as He was (from all eternity) everyday in the state of Sublime Creator." The only difference concerns the idea of creation, which is only to be found in those traditional doctrines that are in some way or other attached to Judaism: fundamentally it is nothing but a particular way of expressing the idea of universal manifestation and its relation with the Principle.

Chapter 4

Purusha and Prakriti

We must now consider *Purusha* no longer in itself, but in relation to manifestation; and this will enable us later on to understand better why it can be regarded under several aspects, while being at the same time one in reality. It may be said then that *Purusha,* in order that manifestation may be produced, must enter into correlation with another principle, although such a correlation is really non-existent in relation to the highest (*uttama*) aspect of *Purusha,* for there cannot in truth be any other principle than the Supreme Principle, except in a relative sense; but once we are dealing, even principally, with manifestation, we are already in the realm of relativity. The correlative of *Purusha* is then *Prakriti,* the undifferentiated primordial substance; it is the passive principle, which is represented as feminine, while *Purusha,* also called *Pumas,* is the active principle, represented as masculine; and these two are the poles of all manifestation, though remaining unmanifested themselves. It is the union of these complementary principles which produces the integral development of the human individual state, and that applies relatively to each individual. Moreover the same may be said of all other manifested states of the being and not only of the human state; for, although we have to consider this state more especially, it is important always to remember that it is but one state among others, and that it is not merely at the confines of human individuality but rather at the confines of the totality of manifested states, in their indefinite multiplicity, that *Purusha* and *Prakriti* appear to us as proceeding in some sort from a polarization of principial Being.

If, instead of considering each individual separately, we consider the whole of a domain formed by a determinate degree of existence, such as the individual domain in which the human state unfolds itself (or not matter what other analogous domain of manifested existence similarly owing its definition to the combination of certain special and limiting conditions), *Purusha* is, for such a domain (including all the beings who develop their corresponding possibilities of manifestation in it, successively as well as simultaneously), identified with *Prajāpati,* the "Lord of produced beings," an expression of *Brahma* Itself insofar as It is conceived as Divine Will and Supreme Ruler.[1] This will is manifested in more particular form, for each special cycle of existence, as the Manu of that cycle, who gives it its Law (*Dharma*). Manu, indeed, as has already been explained elsewhere, must on no account be regarded as a personage or as a "myth", but rather as a principle, which is properly speaking the Cosmic Intelligence, reflected image of *Brahma* (and in reality one with It), expressing itself as the primordial and universal Legislator.[2] Just as Manu is the prototype of man (*mānava*), the pair *Purusha-Prakriti,* relatively to a determinate state of being, may be considered as equivalent, in the realm of existence corresponding to that state, to what Moslem esoterism calls "Universal Man" (*el-Insānul-kāmil*).[3] This conception, moreover, may be further extended to embrace the totality of manifested states and it then establishes the analogy between the constitution of the universal manifestation and that of its individual human modality,[4] or, to adopt the language used by certain Western schools, between the "macrocosm" and the "microcosm."[5]

Now it is essential to notice that the conception of the pair *Purusha-Prakriti* has nothing at all to do with any "dualistic" conception whatsoever, and in particular that it is totally different from the "spirit-matter" dualism of modern Western philosophy, the origin of which is really imputable to Cartesianism. *Purusha* cannot be regarded as corresponding to the philosophical notion of "spirit," as we have already pointed out in connection with the description of *Ātmā* as "Universal Spirit," which term is only acceptable on condition that it is taken in quite a different sense; and despite the assertions of a considerable number of orientalists, *Prakriti* corresponds even less to the notion of "matter", which is in fact so completely foreign to Hindu thought that there is no word in Sanskrit with which to translate it, even approximately; this shows moreover that such a notion is lacking in any real foundation. Furthermore, it is very probable that even the Greeks themselves did not possess the notion of matter as understood by the moderns, philosophers as well as physicists; at any rate the meaning of the word υλη, in Aristotle, is exactly that of "substance" in all its universality, and εἶδος (which is unsatisfactorily rendered by the word "form" on account of the ambiguities to which it too easily gives rise) corresponds no less precisely to "Essence" regarded as the correlative of "Substance." Indeed, these terms "Essence" and "Substance," taken in their widest sense, are perhaps those which give the most exact idea in Western languages of the conception we are discussing, a conception of a much more universal order than that of "spirit" and "matter," and of which the later represents at most but one very particular aspect, a specification referring to one determinate state of being; outside this state it entirely loses its validity and it is in no wise applicable to the whole of universal manifestation, as is the conception of "Essence" and "Substance." It should further be added that the distinction between "Essence" and "Substance," primordial as it is in comparison with all other distinctions, is none the less relative; it is the first of all dualities, that from which all others derive directly or indirectly, and it is with this distinction that multiplicity strictly speaking begins: but one must not see in it the expression of an absolute irreducibility, which is in no wise to be found there: it is Universal Being which, relatively to the manifestation of which it is the Principle, polarizes Itself into "Essence" and "Substance," without Its intrinsic unity being however in any way affected thereby. In this connection it may be pointed out that the Vedānta, from the very fact that it is purely metaphysical, is essentially the "doctrine of non-duality" (*advaita-vāda*);[6] if the Sānkhya has appeared "dualistic" to those people who have failed to understand it, that is because its point of view stops short at the consideration of the first duality, a fact which does not prevent its admitting everything that transcends it as possible, which is the very opposite of what occurs in the case of the systematic conceptions beloved of philosophers.

We have still to define more precisely the nature of *Prakriti,* the first of the twenty-four principles (*tattvas*) enumerated in the Sānkhya; *Purusha,* however, had to be considered before *Prakriti,* since it is inadmissible to endow the plastic or substantial principle (substantial in the strictly etymological sense of the word, meaning the "universal substratum," that is to say, the support of all manifestation)[7] with spontaneity; it is purely potential and passive, capable of every kind of determination, but never determining itself. *Prakriti* cannot therefore really be a cause by itself (we are speaking of "efficient cause"), apart from the action or rather the influence of the essential principle, which is *Purusha,* and which is, so to speak, the "determinant" of manifestation; all manifested things are indeed produced by *Prakriti,* of which they are so many modifications or determinations, but, without the presence of *Purusha,* these productions would be deprived of all reality. The opinion according to which *Prakriti* is self-sufficient as the principle of manifestation could only be derived from an entirely erroneous view of the Sānkhya, originating simply from the fact that, in this doctrine, what is called "production" is always viewed from the standpoint of "Substance,"and perhaps also from the fact that *Purusha* is only mentioned there as the twenty-fifth *tattva,* moreover quite independently of the others, which include *Prakriti* and all its modifications; such an opinion, furthermore, would be formally opposed to the teaching of the Veda.

Mūla Prakriti is "primordial Nature" (in Arabic *el-Fitrah*), the root of all manifestation (since *mūla* signifies "root"); it is also described as *Pradhāna,* that is to say, "that which is laid down before all other things," comprising all determinations potentially; according to the Purānas, it is identified with *Māyā,* conceived as "mother of forms." It is undifferentiated (*avyakta*) and "undistinguishable," neither compounded of parts nor endowed with qualities, inferable from its effects only, since it is imperceptible in itself, and productive without being itself a production. "Root, it is without root, since it would not be a root if it had a root itself."[8] "*Prakriti,* root of all, is not a production. Seven principles, the great (*mahat,* the intellectual principle or *buddhi*) and the others (*ahankāra* or the individual consciousness, which generates the notion of the "ego," and the five *tanmātras* or essential determinations of things) are at the same time productions (of *Prakriti*) and productive (in relation to those which follow). Sixteen (the eleven *indriyas* or faculties of sensation and action, including *manas* or the mental faculty among them, and the five *bhūtas* or substantial and sensible elements) are productions (but unproductive). *Purusha* is neither produced nor productive (in itself),"[9] though it is indeed its action, or rather, according to an expression borrowed from the Far-Eastern tradition, its "actionless activity," which essentially determines everything that is substantially produced through *Prakriti.*[10]

To complete these remarks, it may be added that *Prakriti,* while necessarily one in its "indistinction," contains within itself a triplicity which, on becoming actualized under the "organizing" influence of *Purusha,* gives rise to the multiplicity of determinations. *Prakriti,* in fact, possesses three *gunas* or constitutive qualities, which are in perfect equilibrium in the state of primordial indifferentiation; every manifestation or modification of substance, however, represents a rupture of this equilibrium, and beings in their different states of manifestation participate in the three *gunas* in different degrees and, so to speak, in indefinitely varying proportions. These *gunas* are not therefore, states but conditions of universal Existence, to which all manifested beings are subjected and which must be carefully distinguished from the special conditions which determine and define such and such a state or mode of manifestation. The three *gunas* are: *sattva,* conformity to the pure essence of Being (*Sat*), which is identified with intelligible light or Knowledge and is represented as an upward tendency; *rajas,* the expansive impulse, in accordance with which the being develops itself in a given state, and, so to speak, at a determinate level of existence; and lastly, *tamas,* obscurity, assimilated with ignorance, and represented as a downward tendency. We will confine our remarks in this instance to the foregoing definitions, which we have already mentioned elsewhere; this is not the occasion to enlarge further on these considerations for they lie somewhat outside our present subject, nor to speak of the diverse applications to which they give rise, more especially in relation to the cosmological theory of the elements; these developments will find a more appropriate place in other studies.

References

1. *Prajāpati* is also Vishwakarmā, the "universal constructive principle"; his name and function are moreover capable of various applications, more or less specialised according to whether or not they are referred to the consideration of this or that cycle or determinate state.
2. It is interesting to note that in other traditions the primordial Legislator is also called by names the root of which is the same as that of the Hindu Manu: We have for example *Menes* among the Egyptians and *Minos* among the Greeks; it is therefore a mistake to look upon these names as indicating historical personages.
3. This is the *Adam Qadmon* of the Hebrew *Qabbalah;* it is also the "King" (*Wang*) of the Far-Eastern tradition (*Tao-te-King,* XXV).

4. It is worth remembering that the institution of castes rests essentially upon this analogy. Concerning the function of *Purusha* considered from the point of view we are discussing here, see especially the Purusha-sūkta of the *Rigveda,* X.90. Vishwakarmā, an aspect or function of "Universal Man," corresponds to the "Great Architect of the Universe" of the Western initiations.
5. These terms properly belong to the Hermetic doctrine and are included among those which, in our opinion, may be justifiably employed in spite of the abuse they have been put to by the pseudo-esotericists of the present day.
6. In our *Introduction to the Study of the Hindu Doctrines* it has been explained that this "doctrine of non-duality" must not be confused with "monism"; for whatever from the latter may assume, it always remains a conception simply of a philosophic and not of a metaphysical order. Neither has the "non-dual" doctrine any connection with "pantheism"; it is all the less possible to assimilate these two since the latter denomination, when used in a reasonable sense, always implies a certain "naturalism" which is essentially anti-metaphysical.
7. In order to preclude any possible misinterpretation it should be added that the sense which we here give to "Substance" differs entirely from Spinoza's use of the same term, for, as a result of a "pantheistic" confusion, he employs it in referring to Universal Being Itself, at least as far as he is capable of conceiving It: in reality Universal Being is beyond the distinction of *Purusha* and *Prakriti,* which are unified in It as in their common principle.
8. *Sānkhya-sūtras,* Adhyāya I, sūtra 67.
9. *Sānkhya-kārikā,* shloka 3.
10. Colebrooke (*Essays on the Philosophy of the Hindus*) was right in pointing out the remarkable agreement between the passage just quoted above and the following, taken from the Treatise *De Divisione Naturae* of Scotus Erigena: "It seems to me that the division of Nature must be established according to four different kinds, the first of which is that which creates but is not created; the second, that which is created and itself creates; the third, that which is created and does not create; and lastly the fourth, that which is neither created nor creating" (Book I). "But the first and fourth kind (respectively assimilable to *Prakriti* and to *Purusha*) coincide (are merged or rather are united) in the Divine Nature, for it can be called creative and uncreate, as it is in itself, but also neither creating nor created since, being infinite, it cannot produce anything outside itself and likewise there is no possibility of it not being in itself and by itself" (Book III). It will however be noticed that the idea of "creation" has been substituted for that of "production": furthermore the expression "Divine Nature" is not entirely adequate, since what it here designates is properly speaking Universal Being: in reality it is *Prakriti* which is primordial Nature, while *Purusha,* essentially immutable, stands outside Nature, the very name of which expresses an idea of "becoming."

CHAPTER 5

Purusha unaffected by Individual Modifications

According to the *Bhagavadgītā,* "there are in the world two *Purushas,* the one destructible and the other indestructible; the first is distributed among all beings; the second is immutable. But there is another *Purusha,* the highest (*uttama*), which is called *Paramātmā,* and which, as imperishable Lord, pervades and sustains the three worlds (the earth, the air and the heavens, representing the three fundamental degrees between which all the modes of manifestation are distributed). As I transcend the destructible and even the indestructible (being the Supreme Principle of the one and of the other), I am extolled in the world and in the Veda under the name of *Purushottama.*"[1] Of the first two *Purushas,* the "destructible" is *jīvātmā,* whose separate existence is in fact transitory and contingent like that of the individuality itself; and the "indestructible" is *Ātmā* considered as the Personality, permanent principle of the being through all its states of manifestation;[2] as for the third, it is *Paramātmā,* as the text explicitly declares, of which the Personality is a primordial determination, in accordance with the explanation we have previously given. True as it is to say that the Personality is really beyond the realm of multiplicity, we may nevertheless, in a certain sense, speak of a personality for each being (we refer, naturally, to the being as a whole, and not to one of its states viewed in isolation). That is why the Sānkhya, the point of view of which does not attain to *Purushottama,* often describes *Purusha* as multiple; but it should be noticed that, even in this case, its name is always employed in the singular, so as to emphasise its essential unity. The Sānkhya has nothing in common, therefore, with any "monadism" of the kind association with the name of Leibnitz, where, moreover, it is the "individual substance" which is regarded as a complete whole, forming a sort of closed system, a conception incompatible with any notion of a truly metaphysical order.

Purusha, considered as identical with the personality, "is, so to speak,[3] a portion (*ansha*) of the Supreme Ruler (who, however, is really without parts, being absolutely indivisible and "without duality"), as a spark is a portion of the first (the nature of which is wholly present in every spark)."[4] It is not subject to the conditions which determine the individuality, and even in its relations therewith it remains unaffected by individual modifications (such as pleasure and pain, for example), which are purely contingent and accidental, and not essential to the being, since they all proceed from the plastic principle, *Prakriti* or *Pradhāna,* as from a single root. It is from this substance, containing all the possibilities of manifestation potentially, that modifications are produced in the manifested sphere, by the actual development of these possibilities, or, to use the Aristotelian expression, by their passage from potency to act. "All modification (*parināma*)," says Vijnāna Bhikshu, "from the original production of the world (that is to say, of each cycle of existence) to its final dissolution, proceeds exclusively from *Prakriti* and her derivatives," that is to say from the first twenty-four *tattvas* of the Sānkhya.

Purusha is, however, the essential principle of all things, since it is *Purusha* which determines the development of the possibilities of *Prakriti;* but it never enters itself into manifestation, so that all things, insofar as they are viewed distinctively, are different from it, and nothing which concerns them in their distinctive development (that is to say, in "becoming") can affect its immutability. "Thus the solar or lunar light (capable of manifold modifications) appears identical with that which gives birth to it (the luminous source, considered as immutable in itself), but nevertheless it is distinct therefrom (in its external manifestation; likewise modifications or manifested qualities are, as such, distinct from their essential principle, in that they can in no manner affect it). As the image of the sun reflected in water quivers and fluctuates in accordance with the undulations of the water, yet without affecting the other images reflected therein, much less the solar orb itself, so the modifications of one individual leave other individuals unaffected and, much more so, the Supreme Ruler Himself,"[5] who is *Purushottama,* and with whom the Personality is really identical in its essence, just as all sparks are identical with fire considered as indivisible in its innermost nature.

It is the "living soul" (*jīvātmā*) which is here compared to the image of the sun in water, as being the reflection (*ābhāsa*) in the individual realm and relatively to each individual of the Light, principially one, of the "Universal Spirit" (*Ātmā*); and the luminous ray which confers existence upon this image, connecting it with its source, is as we shall see later on, the higher intellect (*buddhi*), belonging to the realm of formless manifestation.[6] As for the water, which reflects the solar lights, it is habitually regarded as the symbol of the plastic principle (*Prakriti*), the image of "universal passivity"; this symbol, moreover, bearing the same meaning, is common to all traditional doctrines.[7] Here, however, a limitation must be imposed on its general sense, since *buddhi,* although formless and supra-individual, is none the less manifested, and consequently derives from *Prakriti,* of which it is the first production: the water, therefore, can only represent here the potential sum of formal possibilities, or in other words, the realm of manifestation in the individual mode, and thus it leaves outside itself those formless possibilities which, while corresponding with states of manifestation, must none the less be referred to the Universal.[8]

References

1. *Bhagavadgītā,* XV, 16-18.
2. They are "the two birds who dwell on the same tree" according to the text of the Upanishads mentioned in an earlier note. Moreover there is also reference to a tree in the *Katha Upanishad,* Adhyāya II, Valli 6, shruti 1, but in this case the application of the symbol is not longer "microcosmic" but "macrocosmic": "The world is like an everlasting fig-tree (*ashwattha sanātana*) the roots of which point upwards into the air, while the branches grow downwards into the earth, and the hymns of the Veda are its leaves; whosoever knows it, the same knows the Veda." The root is above because it stands for the principle, and the branches are below because they represent the deploying of manifestation; if the figure of the tree is thus seen upside-down, it is because analogy, here as everywhere else, must be applied in an inverse sense. In both cases the tree is described as the sacred fig (*ashwattha* or *pippala*); in this form or in others, the symbolism of the "World-tree" is far from being confined to India: the oak among the Celts, the lime-tree among the Germans, the ash among the Scandinavians, all play exactly the same part.
3. The word *iva* indicates that there is question of a comparison (*upamā*) or of a manner of speech intended to facilitate understanding but which is not to be taken literally. Here is a Taoist text expressing a similar idea: "Norms of every sort, such as that which makes one body of several organs (or one being of several states), ...are so many participations in the Universal Ruler. These participations neither increase Him nor decrease Him, for they are communicated by Him, not

detached from Him" (*Chuangtzu*, chap. II—French translation by Father Wieger, p. 217).

4. *Brahma-sūtras*, Adhyāya II, Pāda 3, sūtra 43. We would remind the reader that in our interpretation we are chiefly following the commentary of Shankarāchārya.
5. *Brahma-sūtras*, Adhyāya II, Pāda 3, sūtras 46-53.
6. It must be pointed out that the ray presupposes a medium of propagation (manifestation in non-individualised mode), and that the image implies a plane of reflection (individualisation under the conditions of a certain state of existence).
7. In this connection one can in particular refer to the opening passage of *Genesis*, I.2: "And the spirit of God moved upon the face of the waters." This passage contains a very clear indication of the two complementary principles we are discussing here, the Spirit corresponding to *Purusha* and the Waters to *Prakriti*. From a different point of view but nevertheless analogically connected with the preceding one, *Ruahh, Elohim* of the Hebrew text can also be assimilated with *Hamsa*, the symbolic swan, the vehicle of Brahmā, which sits on the *Brahmānda*, the "World-egg" that is contained in the primordial Waters; and it must also be noted that *Hamsa* is at the same time the "breath" (*spiritus*), which is the first meaning of *Ruahh* in Hebrew. Lastly, if one adopts the particular point of view of the constitution of the corporeal world, *Ruahh* is Air (*Vāyu*); and, but for the fact that it would imply too long a digression, it would be possible to show that a perfect concordance exists between the *Bible* and the Veda in respect of the development of the sensible elements. In any case, one can discern, in the examples we have already given, an indication of three superposed meanings, referring respectively to the three fundamental degrees of manifestation (formless, subtle and gross) which are described as the "three worlds" (*Tribhuvana*) by the Hindu tradition. These three worlds also figure in the Hebrew *Qabbalah* under the names of *Beriah, Ietsirah* and *Asiah;* over them is *Atsiluth*, which is the principle state of non-manifestation.
8. If the symbol of water is taken in its usual sense, then the sum of formal possibilities is described as the "lower waters" and that of the formless possibilities as the "upper waters." From the point of view of cosmogony, the parting of the "lower waters" from the "upper waters" is also described in *Genesis*, I.6 and 7; it is also worth noting that the word *Maīm*, which means "water" in Hebrew, has the grammatical form of the dual, which, allows of its conveying, among other meanings, the idea of the "double chaos" of the formal and formless possibilities in the potential state. The primordial waters, before their separation, are the totality of the possibilities of manifestation, in so far as the latter constitutes the potential aspect of Universal Being, which is properly speaking *Prakriti*. But there is also another and superior meaning to the same symbolism, which appears when it is carried over beyond Being Itself: the waters then represent Universal Possibility, conceived in an absolutely total manner, that is to say insofar as it embraces at the same time in Its Infinity the domains of manifestation and non-manifestation alike. This last meaning is the highest of all; at the degree immediately below it, in the original polarization of Being, we have *Prakriti*, with which we have still only reached the Principle of manifestation. After that, continuing downwards, the three fundamental degrees of manifestation can be considered as we have done previously: we then have, in the first two cases, the

"double chaos" beforementioned, and lastly, in the corporeal world, water as a sensible element (*ap*), in which capacity it is already included implicitly, like all things that pertain to gross manifestation, in the realm of the "lower waters", for the subtle manifestation plays the part of immediate principle relatively to this gross manifestation. Though the above explanations are somewhat lengthy, we believe they will have served a good purpose in making it easier, by means of the examples given, to understand how a plurality of meaning and applications can be extracted from the traditional texts.

Chapter 6

The Degrees of Individual Manifestation

We must now pass on to consider the different degrees of the manifestation of *Ātmā*, regarded as the Personality, insofar as this manifestation constitutes human individuality; and it may indeed literally be said to constitute it, since this individuality would enjoy no existence at all if it were separated from its principle, that is to say, from the Personality. The expression just used calls, however, for one reservation; by the manifestation of *Ātmā* must be understood manifestation referred to *Ātmā* as its essential principle, but it must not be inferred from this that *Ātmā* manifests itself in some way, since it never enters into manifestation, as we have previously stated, and that is why it is not in any way affected thereby. In other words, *Ātmā* is "That by which all things are manifested, and which is not Itself manifested by anything;"[1] and it is this point which must never be lost sight of throughout all that follows. We will repeat once more that *Ātmā* and *Purusha* are one and the same principle, and that it is from *Prakriti* and not from *Purusha* that all manifestation is produced; but if the Sānkhya, because its point of view is chiefly "cosmological" and not strictly speaking metaphysical, sees this manifestation as the development or "actualization" of the potentialities of *Prakriti,* the Vedānta necessarily sees it quite differently, because it regards *Ātmā,* which is outside any modification or "becoming," as the true principle to which everything must ultimately be referred. It might be said that, viewed in this manner, the Sānkhya and the Vedānta represent respectively the points of view of "Substance" and of "Essence," and that the first can be called a "cosmological" point of view, because it is that of Nature and of "becoming"; but, on the other hand, metaphysic does not limit itself to "Essence" regarded as the correlative of "Substance," nor even to Being, in which these two terms are unified; it extends much further, since it attains to *Paramātmā* or *Purushottama,* which is the Supreme *Brahma,* and therefore its point of view (assuming that such an expression is still applicable here) is truly unlimited.

Furthermore, when we speak of the different degrees of individual manifestation, it should be readily understood that they correspond with the degrees of universal manifestation, by reason of the basic analogy between the "macrocosm" and the "microcosm" to which we have already alluded. This will be still better understood if one remembers that all manifested beings alike are subject to the general conditions which limit the states of existence in which they are placed; if we cannot, when considering any given being, really isolate one state of that being from the whole composed of all the other states among which it is situated hierarchically at a given level, no more can we, from another point of view, isolate that state from all that belongs, not to the same being, but to the same degree of universal Existence; and thus all appears linked together in various different ways, both within manifestation itself, and also insofar as the latter, forming a single whole in its indefinite multiplicity, is attached to its principle, that is, to Being, and through Being to the Supreme Principle. Multiplicity, once it is a possibility, exists according to its own mode, but this mode is illusory, in the sense we have already ascribed to that word (that of a lesser reality), because the very existence of this multiplicity is based upon unity, from which it is derived and within which it is principially contained. When viewing the whole of universal manifestation in this manner, we may say that in the very multiplicity of its degrees and of its modes "Existence is unique," according to a formula borrowed from Moslem esoterism; furthermore there is a fine distinction which it is important to note here as between "unicity" and "unity": the first embraces multiplicity as such while the second is its principle (not its "root," in the sense in which this word is applied to *Prakriti* only, but as containing within itself, "essentially" as well as "substantially," all the possibilities of manifestation). It can therefore correctly be said that Being is one, and that it is Unity itself[2]—in the metaphysical sense, however, and not in the mathematical sense, for at this stage we have passed quite outside the domain of quantity. Between metaphysical Unity and mathematical unity there is analogy but not identity; and similarly, when we speak of the multiplicity of universal manifestation, it is again not with a quantitative multiplicity that we are concerned, for quantity is merely a special condition of certain manifested states. Finally, if Being is one, the Supreme Principle is "without duality," as we shall see in what follows: Unity is indeed the first of all determinations, but it is already a determination, and, as such, it cannot properly be applied to the Supreme Principle.

Having given these few indispensable explanations, let us return to the consideration of the degrees of manifestation. It is necessary, as we have seen, to draw a distinction first of all between formless and formal manifestation; but when we confine our attention to the individuality, it is always exclusively with the latter that we are concerned. The human state properly so called, like every other individual state, belongs wholly to formal manifestation, since it is precisely the presence of form among the conditions contributing to make up a particular mode of existence which characterizes that mode as individual. If, therefore, we have to consider a formless element, it will also necessarily be a supra-individual element, and, as regards its relationship with human individuality, it must never be considered as constitutive of it, nor for any reason at all as forming a part of it, but as linking the individuality to the Personality. The Personality, indeed, is unmanifested, even insofar as it is regarded more especially as the principle of the manifested states, just as Being, although it is properly the principle of universal manifestation, remains outside of and beyond that manifestation (and we may recall Aristotle's "motionless mover" at this point); on the other hand, formless manifestation is also, in a relative sense, principial in relation to formal manifestation, and thus it establishes a link between the latter and its higher unmanifested principle, which is, moreover, the common principle of these two orders of manifestation. Similarly, if we distinguish, in formal or individual manifestation, between the subtle and the gross state, the first is, more relatively still, principial in relation to the second, and consequently it is placed hierarchically between it and formless manifestation. We have therefore, through a series of principles becoming progressively more relative and determined, a chain at once logical and ontological (the two points of view, moreover, corresponding in such a way that they can only be separated artificially) extending from the unmanifested downward to gross manifestation, passing through the intermediary of formless manifestation and then of subtle manifestation; and, whether we are dealing with the "macrocosm" or with the "microcosm", such is general order which must be followed in the development of the possibilities of manifestation.

The elements about which we shall now be speaking are the *tattvas* enumerated by the Sānkhya, with the exception, of course, of the first and the last, that is, of *Prakriti* and *Purusha.* We have seen that, among these *tattvas,* some are regarded as "productive productions" and others as "unproductive production:" a question therefore suggests itself in this connection: is this division equivalent to the division we have just specified in respect of the degrees of manifestation, or does it not at least roughly correspond with it? For Example, if we limit ourselves to the point of view of individuality, we might be inclined to refer the *tattvas* of the first group to the subtle state and those of the second to the gross state, the more so since, in a certain sense, subtle manifestation is productive of gross manifestation, while the latter is not productive of any further state: but the answer is not really quite so simple. In point of fact, in the first group we have *buddhi* first of all, which is the formless element to which we were alluding just now; as to the other *tattvas* which are included with it, *ahankāra* and the *tanmātras,* they do indeed belong to the domain of subtle manifestation. Again, in the second group, the *bhūtas* incontestably belong to the domain of gross manifestation, since they are the corporeal elements: but *manas,* not being corporeal, must, in itself at least, be referred to subtle manifestation, although its activity is also exercised in relation to gross manifestation; while the other *indriyas* have in some sort a twofold aspect, being conceivable at the same time as faculties and as organs, psychically as well as corporeally therefore, which is also to say both in the subtle and in the gross state. It must, moreover, be clearly understood that that part of subtle manifestation which is taken into consideration in all these circumstances is really only the portion affecting the human individual state in its extra-corporeal modality; and, superior as these may be to the corporeal modality, inasmuch as they contain its immediate principle (their domain extending at the same time much further), nevertheless, if we situate them in the totality of universal Existence, they still belong to that degree of Existence in which the human state as a whole is situated. The same remark also applies when we say that subtle manifestation is productive of gross manifestation: for this to be strictly accurate however, it is necessary, in the case of the former, to apply the restriction we have just mentioned, since the same relationship cannot be established in respect of those other states which, though likewise individual states, are not human states and therefore differ entirely as to their conditions (other than the condition imposed by the presence of form); for those states must nevertheless also be included in subtle manifestation, as we have already explained, from the moment that we accept the human individuality as a term of comparison as we must inevitably do, while clearly bearing in mind that the human individual state is really neither more nor less important than any other state whatsoever.

One last observation is called for; in speaking of the order of development of the possibilities of manifestation, or of the order in which the elements corresponding to the different phases of this development should be enumerated, great care must be taken to explain that such an order implies a purely logical succession, signifying, however, a real ontological connection, and that there cannot be any question at all here of a temporal succession. Development in time, indeed, only corresponds with a special condition of existence, which is one of those conditions defining the domain in which the human state is contained; and there are an indefinite number of other modes of development equally possible, and included also within universal manifestation. Human individuality cannot therefore be related in the order of time to other states of the being, since these, in a general way, are extra-temporal: and that is also true even when it is only a question of states which likewise belong to formal manifestation. It might further be added that certain extensions of the human individuality, outside its corporeal modality, are already freed from time, without on that account being exempt from the general conditions of the state to which this individuality belongs; these extensions are really situated in mere prolongations of that state, and we shall doubtless in other studies have occasion to explain just how such prolongations may be reached through the suppression of one or other of the conditions which together contribute to make up the corporeal world. Such being the case, it is all the more apparent that there cannot be any question of the temporal condition applying outside this same state, nor, consequently, of its governing the relation of the integral human state with other states; and this is even less admissible when it is a question of a principle common to all the states of manifestation, or of an element which, though indeed manifested, is nevertheless superior to all formal manifestation, as is the element which we have to consider next.

References

1. *Kena Upanishad*, Khanda I, shrutis 5-9; the whole passage will be given in a subsequent chapter.
2. The same idea is expressed by the scholastic adage: *Esse et unum convertuntur.*

CHAPTER 7

Buddhi or the Higher Intellect

The first degree of the manifestation of *Ātmā,* taking this expression in the sense explained in the last chapter, is the higher intellect (*buddhi*), which, as we have seen above, is also called *mahat* or the "great principle"; it is the second of the twenty-five principles of the Sānkhya, and the first therefore of all the productions of *Prakriti.* This principle still pertains to the universal order, since it is formless; we must not, however, forget that it already belongs to manifestation, and therefore proceeds from *Prakriti,* for all manifestation, at whatever degree we take it, necessarily implies the two correlative and complementary terms, *Purusha* and *Prakriti,* "Essence" and "Substance." It is none the less true that *buddhi* transcends the domain not only of human individuality but of every individual state whatsoever, and it is this which justifies its other name of *mahat:* it is never really individualized therefore, and it is not until the next stage, that of the particular (or rather "particularist") consciousness of the "ego," that we shall find individuality realized.

Buddhi, considered in relation to the human individuality or to any other individual state, is, then, its immediate but transcendent principle, just as, from the point of view of universal Existence, formless manifestation is the principle of formal manifestation; and it is at the same time what may be called the expression of the Personality in manifestation, therefore that which unifies the being throughout the indefinite multiplicity of its individual state (the human state, in its utmost extension, being but one state among all the rest). In other words, if we view the "Self" (*Ātmā*), or Personality, as the Spiritual Sun[1] which shine at the centre of the entire being, *buddhi* will be the ray directly emanating from this Sun and illuminating in its entirety the particular individual state that more especially concerns us, while at the same time linking it to the other individual states of the same being, or rather, more generally still, to all the manifested states (individual or non-individual) of that being, and, beyond these, to the centre itself. Furthermore it should be remarked here, without however going into the question so far as to interrupt the course of our exposition, that, owing to the fundamental unity of the being in all its states, the centre of each state, where this spiritual ray is projected, should be regarded as virtually, if not effectively, identified with the centre of the entire being; and it is for this reason that any state whatsoever, the human state as well as any other, can be taken as a basis for the realization of the Supreme Identity. It is precisely in this sense, and in virtue of this identification, that one may say, as we did in the first place, that *Purusha* itself dwells at the centre of the human individuality, that is to say, at the point where the intersection of the spiritual ray with the realm of the vital possibilities determines the "living soul" (*jīvātmā*).[2]

Furthermore *buddhi,* like everything that proceeds from the potentialities of *Prakriti,* participates in the three *gunas;* that explains why, when viewed from the standpoint of distinctive knowledge (*vijnāna*), it is regarded as ternary, and in the sphere of universal Existence, it is then identified with the divine *Trimūrti;* "*Mahat* is conceived distinctively as three Gods (in the sense of three aspects of the intelligible Light, for this is the real meaning of the Sanskrit word *deva,* of which the Latin word *deus* is, moreover, etymologically the exact equivalent),[3] through the influence of the three *gunas,* being one single manifestation (*murti*) in three Gods. In the universal order, it is the Divinity (*Īshwara,* not in Himself, but under His three principal aspects as Brahmā, Vishnu, and Shiva, constituting the *Trimurti,* or "triple manifestation"); but regarded distributively (under the aspect of "separativity," which is, moreover, purely contingent) it belongs (without however being itself individualized) to individual beings (to whom it communicates the possibility of participating in the divine attributes, that is to say, in the very nature of Universal Being, the Principle of all existence)."[4] It is easy to see that *buddhi* is here considered in its respective relations with the first two of the three *Purushas* which are spoken of in the *Bhagavadgītā:* in the "macrocosmic" order the "immutable" *Purusha* is *Īshwara* Himself, of whom the *Trimurti* is the expression in manifested mode (we are speaking, of course, of formless manifestation, for there is nothing individual about it); and it is stated that the other *Purusha* is "disseminated among all beings." Similarly, in the "microcosmic" order, *buddhi* may be viewed relatively to the Personality (*Ātmā*) and relatively to the "living soul" (*jīvātmā*), the latter moreover only being the reflection of the Personality in the individual human state, a reflection which could not exist without the mediation of *buddhi*. To recall here the symbol of the sun and its reflected image in the water, *buddhi* is, as we have stated, the ray which determines the formation of the image and at the same time unites it with its luminous source.

It is in virtue of the twofold relationship which has just been indicated, and of this function of intermediary between the Personality and the individuality, that we may regard the intellect, in spite of the inevitable inadequacy of such a way of speaking, as passing in some sort from the state of universal potentiality to the individualized state, but without really ceasing to be such as it was, since this apparent passage only comes about through its intersection with the particular domain constituted by certain conditions of existence defining the individuality in question; as a resultant of this intersection it then produces the individual consciousness (*ahankāra*), implied in the "living soul" (*jīvātmā*) in which it is inherent. As we have already pointed out, this consciousness, which is the third principle of the Sānkhya, gives rise to the notion of the "ego" (*aham*, whence the name *ahankāra*, literally "that which makes the me"), since its proper function is to establish the individual conviction (*abhimāna*), that is to say, precisely the notion that "I am" concerned with external (*bāhya*) and internal (*abhyantara*) objects, which are respectively of objects of perception (*pratyaksha*) and contemplation (*dhyāna*); and the sum total of these objects is described by the term *idam*, "this," when it is thus conceived as in opposition to *aham* or "me," a purely relative opposition, however, and for that reason quite different from that which modern philosophers claim to establish between "subject" and "object" or between "mind" and "things." Thus the individual consciousness proceeds directly, but simply as a conditioned modality, from the intellectual principle, and, in its turn, produces all the other principles or elements specially attaching to the human individuality. These elements we shall now consider in greater detail.

References

1. As to sense in which this expression should be taken, we would refer the reader to the remark previously made concerning the "Universal Spirit."
2. Clearly we are not referring in this instance to a mathematical point, but to what might by analogy be called a metaphysical point, always with the proviso however that such an expression must not be allowed to evoke the notion of the "monad" of Leibnitz, since *jīvātmā* is noting more than a particular and contingent manifestation of *Ātmā,* so that it separate existence is really illusory. The geometrical symbolism referred to will however be set forth in a separate work, together with all the developments to which it lends itself.
3. Were one to give to the word "God" the meaning that it has subsequently assumed in Western languages, its use in the plural would make nonsense from the Hindu just as much as from the Christian or Moslem point of view, since, as we pointed out before, it could then only apply to *Īshwara* exclusively, in His indivisible unity which is that of Universal Being, whatever multiplicity of aspects can be considered as pertaining to it in a secondary way.
4. *Matsya Purāna.* It will be noticed that *buddhi* is not unrelated to the *Logos* of the Alexandrians.

CHAPTER 8

Manas or the Inward Sense: The Ten External Faculties of Sensation and Action

In its list of the *tattvas,* after individual consciousness (*ahankāra*), the Sānkhya goes on to describe the five *tanmātras,* subtle elementary determinations, incorporeal therefore and outwardly imperceptible, belonging to the same group of productive productions. In an immediate sense they constitute respectively the principles of the five *bhūtas* or corporeal and sensible elements and receive their definite expression in the particular conditions of individual existence prevailing at the level of the human state. The word *tanmātra* literally means an "assignment" (*mātra,* measure, determination) delimiting the proper sphere of a given quality (*tad* or *tat,* neuter pronoun, "that," taken here in the sense of "quiddity," like the Arabic *dāt*)[1] in universal Existence; but this is not the place to enter into fuller details on this subject. We will merely remark that the five *tanmātras* are usually indicated by the names of the sensible qualities: auditive or sonorous (*shabda*), tangible (*sparsha*), visible (*rūpa,* with the double sense of form and colour), sapid (*rasa*), olfactory (*gandha*); but these qualities must be looked upon here as existing in a relatively principal and "non-developed" state only, since it is through the *bhūtas* alone that they will be actually manifested in the sensible order; furthermore the relation of the *tanmātras* to the *bhūtas* is analogous, in its relative degrees, to that of "Essence" to "Substance," so that the term "elementary essences" could be applied accurately enough to the *tanmātras.*[2] The five *bhūtas,* in the order of their production or of their manifestation (an order parallel to that just indicated for the *tanmātras,* since a corresponding sensible quality goes with each element) are Ether (*Ākāsha*), Air (*Vāyu*), Fire (*Tejas*), Water (*Ap*) and Earth (*Prithvī* or *Prithivī*): and it is from these that the whole of gross or corporeal manifestation is made up.

Between the *tanmātras* and the *bhūtas,* and constituting with the latter the group of "unproductive productions," there are eleven distinct and specifically individual faculties, which proceed from *ahankāra,* and which, at the same time, all participate in the five *tanmātras.* Of the eleven faculties in question ten are external, five of sensation and five of action; the eleventh, which is concerned with both these functions, is the inward sense or mental faculty (*manas*), and this is directly attached to consciousness (*ahankāra*).[3] It is to *manas* that we must refer individual thought, which belongs to the formal order (and which includes reason as well as memory and imagination);[4] it is in no way inherent in the transcendent intellect (*buddhi*), the attributes of which are essentially formless. It is worth remarking in this connection that, for Aristotle also, pure intellect is of a transcendent order and can claim knowledge of universal principles as its proper object; this knowledge, which is not discursive in any respect, is acquired directly and immediately by intellectual intuition. To avoid any misunderstanding it should be added that this intuition has nothing at all to do with the so-called "intuition" of a merely sensitive and vital order, which plays such a prominent part in the decidedly anti-metaphysical theories of certain contemporary philosophers.

As for the development of the different faculties of individual man, it is enough to quote the teaching of the *Brahma-sūtras* on this subject: "The intellect, the inward sense, and also the faculties of sensation and action, are developed (in manifestation) and re-absorbed (into the unmanifested) in a similar sequence (except that re-absorption proceeds in an inverse order to that of development),[5] and this sequence always follows that of the elements from which these faculties proceed as regards their constitution[6] (with the exception, however, of the intellect, which is developed in the formless order prior to the determination of any formal or properly individual principle). As a *Purusha* (or *Ātmā*), its emanation (insofar as it is regarded as the Personality of a being) is not a birth (even in the widest meaning of the word),[7] neither is it a production (implying a starting-point for its actual existence, as is the case for everything that proceeds from *Prakriti*). One cannot in fact assign to it any limitation (by any particular condition of existence), since, being identified with the Supreme *Brahma,* it partakes of Its infinite essence[8] (implying the possession of the divine attributes, at least virtually and even actually insofar as this participation is effectively realised in the Supreme Identity, not to speak of all that lies beyond any attribution whatsoever, since here we are contemplating the Supreme *Brahma,* which is *Nirguna,* and nor merely *Brahma* as *Saguna,* that is to say *Īshwara*).[9] It is active, but only in principle therefore "actionless"),[10] for this activity (*kartritva*) is not essential to it nor inherent in it, but is simply eventual and contingent (merely relative to its states of manifestation). As the carpenter, grasping in his hand his axe and his other tools and then laying them aside, enjoys tranquillity and repose, so this *Ātmā,* in its union with its instruments (by means of which its principal faculties are expressed and developed in each of its states of manifestation, and which are thus nothing but the manifestations of these faculties with their respective organs), is active (although this activity in no way affects its inmost nature), and, in relinquishing them, enjoys repose and tranquillity (in the 'inaction' from which, in itself, it never departed)."[11]

"The various faculties of sensation and action (indicated by the word *prāna* in a secondary acceptation) are eleven in number: five of sensation (*buddhīndriyas* or *jnānendriyas,* means or instruments of knowledge in their own particular sphere), five of action (*karmendriyas*), and the inward sense (*manas*). Where a greater number (thirteen) is given, the term *indriya* is employed in its widest and most comprehensive sense, distinguishing within *manas,* by reason of the plurality of its functions, the intellect (not in itself and insofar as it belongs to the transcendent order, but as a particular determination relative to the individual), the individual consciousness (*ahankāra,* from which *manas* cannot be separated), and the inward sense properly so called (what the scholastic philosophers term "*sensorium commune*"). Where a lesser number (usually seven) is given, the same term is applied in a more restricted manner: thus, seven sensible organs are specified, the two eyes, the two ears, the two nostrils and the mouth or tongue (so that, in this case, we are dealing merely with the seven openings or orifices of the head). The eleven faculties mentioned above (although indicated collectively by the term *prāna*) are not (as are the five *vāyus* of which we shall speak later) simple modifications of the *mukhya-prāna* or principal vital act (respiration, with the assimilation ensuing from it), but distinct principles (from the special point of view of human individuality)."[12]

The term *prāna* in its most usual acceptation, really means "vital breath"; but in certain Vedic texts, it serves to describe something which, in the universal sense, is identified in principle with *Brahma* Itself, as when it is said that in deep sleep (*sushupti*), all the faculties are re-absorbed into *prāna,* since "while a man sleeps without dreaming, his spiritual principle (*Ātmā* viewed in relation to him) is one with *Brahma,*"[13] this state being beyond distinction and therefore truly supra-individual: that is why the word *swapiti,* "he sleeps," is interpreted as *swam apīto bhavati,* "he has entered into his own (Self)."[14]

As to the word *indriya,* it really means "power" which is also the primary meaning of the word "faculty"; but, by extension, it comes to mean, as has already been pointed out, both the faculty and its bodily organ, which are thus described by one and the same word and which are considered as constituting in combination a single instrument, either of knowledge (*buddhi* or *jnāna,* these terms being here taken in their widest sense), or of action (*karma*). The five instruments of sensation are: the ears or hearing (*shrotra*), the skin or touch (*twach*), the eyes or sight (*chakshus*), the tongue or taste (*rasana*), the nose or smell (*ghrāna*), being enumerated thus in the order of development of the senses, which is that of the corresponding elements (*bhūtas*); but, to explain this correspondence in detail, it would be necessary to discuss fully the conditions of corporeal existence, which we cannot undertake to do here. The five instruments of action are: the organs of excretion (*pāyu*), the generative organs (*upastha*), the hands (*pāni*), the feet (*pāda*) and lastly the voice or organ of speech (*vāch*),[15] which is reckoned as the tenth. *Manas* must be regarded as the eleventh, fulfilling in its own nature a double function of service both towards perception and towards action, and partaking in consequence of the properties of each, which it centralizes to a certain extent within itself.[16]

According to the Sānkhya, these faculties with their respective organs are (distinguishing three faculties in *manas*) the thirteen instruments of knowledge in the sphere of human individuality (for the end of action is not in action itself but only insofar as it relates to knowledge): three are internal and ten external, compared to three sentinels and ten gates (consciousness being inherent in the former, but not in the latter when viewed distinctively). A bodily sense perceives, and an organ of action executes (the one being, as it were, an "entry" and the other an "outgoing": there are here two successive and complementary phases, of which the first is a centripetal and the second a centrifugal movement); between the two, the inward sense (*manas*) examines; consciousness (*ahankāra*) makes the individual application, that is to say the assimilation of the perception by the "ego," of which it henceforth becomes part as a secondary modification; and, finally, the pure intellect (*buddhi*) transposes the data of the preceding faculties into the Universal.

REFERENCES

1. It should be noted that these words *tat* and *dāt* are phonetically equivalent to one another, as also to be English *that* which bears the same meaning.
2. It is in a sense closely resembling this conception of the *tanmātras* that Fabre d'Olivet, in his interpretation of *Genesis (la Langue hébraique restitutée)*, makes use of the expression "intelligible elementisation."
3. Concerning the production of these various principles, considered from the "macrocosmic" point of view, cp., *Mānava Dharma-shāstra* (The Law of Manu), Adhyāya I, shlokas 14-20.
4. This was doubtless Aristotle's meaning when he said that "man (as an individual) never thinks without images," that is to say without forms.
5. The reader must be reminded that it is in no wise an order to temporal succession that is in question.
6. Here the reference can be either to the *tanmātras* or the *bhūtas*, depending on whether the *indriyas* are considered in the subtle or the gross state, that is to say as faculties or as organs.
7. It is possible, in fact, to apply the name of "birth" or "death" to the beginning and end of any cycle whatsoever, that is to say, of an existence in whatever state of manifestation, and not in the human state alone; as will be explained further on, the passage from one state to another is then both a death and a birth, according as it is taken in relation to the antecedent or to the subsequent state.
8. The word "essence," when it is thus applied analogically, ceases to be in any way a correlative of "substance"; besides, whatever possesses a correlative of any kind cannot be infinite. Similarly, the word "nature" when applied to Universal Being or even beyond Being, loses its usual and etymological meaning entirely, together with the idea of "becoming" which is implied in it.
9. The possession of the divine attributes is called in Sanskrit *aishwarya* a constituting a real "connaturality" with *Īshwara.*
10. Aristotle was right in also stressing the point that the prime mover of all things (or the principle of movement) must itself be motionless, which amounts to saying, in other words, that the principle of all action must be "actionless."
11. *Brahma-sūtras,* Adhyāya II, Pāda 3, sūtras 14-17 and 33-40.
12. Ibid., Pāda 4, sūtras 1-7.

13. Commentary of Shankarāchārya on the *Brahma-sūtras*, Adyāya III, Pāda 2, sūtra 7.
14. *Chhāndogya Upanishad*, Prapāthaka VI, Khanda VIII, shruti 1. It goes without saying that this is a case of interpretation by the method of *nirukta* and not one of etymological derivation.
15. This word *vāch* is identical with the Latin *vox*.
16. *Mānava Dharma-shāstra*, Adhyāya II, shlokas 89-92.

CHAPTER 9

The Envelopes of the "Self"; the Five Vāyus or Vital Functions

Purusha or *Ātmā,* manifesting itself as *jīvātmā* in the living form of the individual being, is regarded, according to the Vedānta, as clothing itself in a series of "envelopes" (*koshas*) or successive vehicles, representing so many phases of its manifestation; it would be altogether wrong, however, to compare these envelopes to "bodies", since it is the last phase only that belongs to the corporeal order. It is important to note, moreover, that *Ātmā* cannot, strictly speaking, be said to be actually contained within such envelopes, since, by its very nature, it is not susceptible of any limitation and is in no way conditioned by any state of manifestation whatsoever.[1]

The first envelope (*ānandamaya-kosha,* the suffix *maya* signifying "made of" or "consisting of" whatever is denoted by the word to which it is joined) is none other than the totality of the possibilities of manifestation which *Ātmā* comprises within itself, in its "permanent actuality" in the principial and undifferentiated state. It is called "made of Beatitude" (*ānanda*), because the "Self," in this primordial state, enjoys the plenitude of its own being, and it is in no way really distinct from the "Self"; it is superior to conditioned existence, which presupposes it, and it is situated at the level of pure Being; that is why it is regarded as characteristic of *Īshwara.*[2] Here, therefore, we are in the formless order; it is only when this envelope is viewed in relation to formal manifestation, and insofar as the principle of the latter is contained in it, that it can be said to represent principial or causal from (*kārana-sharīra*), that by which form will be manifested and actualized in the succeeding stages.

The second envelope (*vijnānamaya-kosha*) is formed by the directly reflected Light (in the intelligible sense) of integral and universal Knowledge (*jnāna,* the particle *vi* implying the distinctive mode);[3] it is composed of five "elementary essences" (*tanmātras*), "conceivable" but not "perceptible," in their subtle state; and it arises out of the conjunction of the higher intellect (*buddhi*) with the principial faculties of perception proceeding respectively from the five *tanmātras,* and the external development of which constitutes the five senses of the corporeal individual.[4] The third envelope (*manomaya-kosha*), in which the constituents of the preceding envelope are linked up with the inward sense (*manas*), especially brings into play the mental consciousness[5] or thinking faculty; this, as we have previously explained, belongs exclusively to the individual and formal order, and its development arises from the radiation, in reflective mode, of the higher intellect within a determinate individual state, which is in this case the human state. The fourth envelope (*prānamaya-kosha*) comprises the faculties which proceed from the "vital breath" (*prāna*), that is to say, the five *vāyus* (modalities of this *prāna*), as well as the faculties of action and sensation (these last already existing principially in the two preceding envelopes as purely "conceptive" faculties, at which stage, indeed, there could be no question of any sort of action, any more than of any external perception). The combination of these last envelopes (*vijnānamaya, manomaya* and *prānamaya*) constitutes the subtle from (*sūkshma-sharīra* or *linga-sharīra*), as opposed to the gross or corporeal form (*sthūla-sharīra*); thus we meet again here with the distinction between the two modes of formal manifestation which we have referred to on several previous occasions.

The five vital functions or actions are called *vāyus,* although they are no strictly speaking air or wind (which is the general meaning of the word *vāyu* or *vāta,* derived from the root *vā,* to go, to move, and usually denoting the element air, one of the characteristic properties of which is mobility),[6] since they belong to the subtle and not to the corporeal state; as we have said above, they are modalities of the "vital breath" (*prāna,* or more generally *ana*)[7] considered chiefly in relation to respiration. They are: (1) aspiration, that is, respiration regarded as ascending in its initial phase (*prāna,* in the strictest sense of this word), and attracting the still unindividualized elements of the cosmic environment, causing them to participate, by assimilation, in the individual consciousness; (2) inspiration, considered as descending in a succeeding phase (*apāna*), whereby these elements penetrate into the individuality; (3) a phase intermediary between the two preceding one (*vyāna*), consisting, on the one hand, of all the reciprocal actions and reactions which are produced upon the contact of the individual with the surrounding elements and, on the other hand, of the various resultant vital movements, of which the circulation of the blood is the corresponding movement in the bodily organism; (4) expiration (*udāna*), which projects the breath, while transforming it, beyond the limits of the restricted individuality (that is, the individuality reduced simply to those modalities which are commonly developed in all men) into the sphere of the possibilities of the extended individuality, viewed in its integrality;[8] (5) digestion, or inner substantial assimilation (*samāna*), bu which the elements absorbed become an integral part of the individuality.[9] It is clearly stated that all this is not purely a matter of the operation of one or of several bodily organs; it is, in fact, easy to realize that it refers not merely to the analogically corresponding physiological functions, but rather to vital assimilation in the widest possible sense.

The corporeal or gross form (*sthūla-sharīra*) is the fifth and last envelope, the one which, for the human state, corresponds to the most external mode of manifestation; it is the alimentary envelope (*annamaya-kosha*), composed of the five sensible elements (*bhūtas*) out of which all bodies are constituted. It assimilates to itself the combined elements received in nutriment (*anna,* a word derived from the verbal rood *ad* to eat),[10] secreting the finer parts, which remain in the organic circulation, and excreting or rejecting the coarser, excepting those however which are deposited in the bones. As a result of this assimilation the earthy substances become the flesh, the watery substances, the blood, and the igneous substances, the fat, the marrow and the nervous systems (phosphoric matter); for there are corporeal substances in which the nature of one element or another predominates, although they are all formed by the union of the five elements.[11]

Every organic being, dwelling in such a bodily form, possesses, in a more or less complete degree of development, the eleven individual faculties of which we have spoken above, and as we have also seen, these faculties are manifested in the bodily organism by means of the eleven corresponding organs (*avayavas,* a name which is also applied in the subtle state, but only by analogy with the gross state). According to Shankarāchārya,[12] three classes of organic beings may be distinguished, according to their mode of reproduction: (1) the viviparous (*jīvaja,* or *yonija,* or again, *jarāyuja*), such as man and the other mammals; (2) the oviparous (*āndaja*), such as birds, reptiles, fish and insects; (3) the germiniparous (*udbhijja*) which includes both the lower animals and plants, the former mobile, being born chiefly in water, while the latter which are immobile are usually born in the earth; however, according to sundry passages in the Veda, nutriment (*anna*), that is to say vegetation (*oshadhi*) also proceeds from water, since it is rain (*varsha*) which fertilizes the earth.[13]

References

1. In the *Taittirīya Upanishad*, Valli II, Anuvāka 8, shruti 1, and Valli III, Anuvāka 10, shruti 5, the designations of the various envelopes are referred directly to the "Self", according as it is considered in relation to this or that state of manifestation.
2. Whereas the other designations (those of the four following envelopes) can be considered as applicable to *jīvātmā*, the envelope called *ānandamaya* applies not only to *Īshawara* but also, by transposition, even to *Paramātmā* or the Supreme *Brahma* and that is why it is said in the *Taittirīya Upanishad*, Valli II, Anuvāka 5, shruti 1: "Differing from that which consists of distinctive knowledge (*vijnānamaya*) is the other interior Self (*anyo'ntara Ātmā*) which consists of Bliss (*ānandamaya*)." Cp. *Brahma-sūtras* Adhyāya I, Pāda 1, sūtras 12-19.
3. The Sanskrit word *jñāna* has the selfsame root as the Greek Γνωσις, which it also shares with the Latin *co-gnoscere;* it expresses an idea of "production" or "generation" because the being "becomes" whatever it knows and realizes itself through that knowledge.
4. It is starting from this second envelope that the term *sharīra* properly applies, especially if this word, as interpreted by the methods of *nirukta,* be given the sense of "dependent upon the six (principles)," that is to say upon *buddhi* (or upon *ahankāra* which is derived directly from it and is the first principle in the individual order) and the five *tanmātras* (*Mānava Dharma-shāstra,* Adhyāya I, shloka 17.
5. By this expression we mean something representing a more advanced degree of determination than individual consciousness pure and simple: it might be said to be the resultant of the union of *manas* and *ahankāra.*
6. We refer the reader to the previous footnote concerning the various applications of the Hebrew word *ruahh,* which corresponds fairly closely to the Sanskrit *vāyu.*
7. The root *an* occurs again, with similar meaning, in the Greek ανεμος, "breath" or "wind" and in the Latin *anima,* "soul," the original and proper meaning of which is precisely "vital breath."
8. It should be observed that the word "expire" means both "to eject the breath" (in respiration) and "to die" (in respect of the bodily part of the human individuality); both these meanings are related to the *udāna* in question.
9. *Brahma-sūtras,* Adhyāya II, Pāda 4, sūtras 8-13. Cp. *Chhāndogya Upanishad,* Prapāthaka V, Khandas 19-23; *Maitri Upanishad,* Prapāthaka, II, shruti 6.
10. This root is the same as that of the Latin *edere,* and also, though in more altered form, that of the English "eat" and the German *essen.*

11. *Brahma-sūtras,* Adhyāya II, Pāda 4, sūtra 21. Cp. *Chhāndogya Upanishad,* Prapāthaka 6, Khanda 5, shrutis 1-3.
12. Commentary on the *Brahma-sūtras,* Adhyāya III, Pāda 1, sūtras 20 and 21. Cp. *Chhāndogya Upanishad,* Prapāthaka VI, Khanda 3, shruti 1; also *Aitareya Upanishad,* Khanda V, shruti 3. The later text, besides the three classes of living beings mentioned in the others, mentions a fourth class, namely those born of damp heat (*swedaja*); but this class can be linked on to the seed-born class.
13. See especially *Chhāndogya Upanishad,* Prapāthaka I, Khanda 1, shruti 2: "Vegetables are the essence (*rasa*) of water" Prapāthaka 5, Khanda 6, shruti 2 and Prapāthaka 7, Khanda 4, shruti 2: *anna* arises or proceeds from *varsha.* The word *rasa* literally means "sap" and it has been seen earlier on that it also signifies "taste" or "savour"; moreover in French also the words *sève* and *saveur,* like the corresponding English words, have the same root (*sap*) which is at the same time that of the Latin *sapere* (French *savoir*) by reason of the analogy which exists between nutritive assimilation in the bodily order and cognitive assimilation in the mental and intellectual orders. It should also be noted that the word *anna* sometimes refers to the elements earth itself, which is the last in the order of development, and which is also derived from the element water which immediately precedes it (*Chhāndogya Upanishad,* Prapāthaka VI, Khanda 2, shruti 4).

CHAPTER 10

The Essential Unity and Identity of the "Self" in all the States of the Being

At this stage it is necessary to emphasise a point of fundamental importance. All the principles or elements we have been speaking about, which are described as distinct, are indeed so when viewed from the individual standpoint, but only from that standpoint, for in reality they merely constitute so many manifested modalities of the "Universal Spirit" (*Ātmā*). In other words, although accidental and contingent insofar as they are manifested, they serve as the expression of certain essential possibilities of *Ātmā* (those which, from their very nature, are possibilities of manifestation); and these possibilities, in principle and in their basic reality, are in no wise distinct from *Ātmā*. This is why they must be considered, in the Universal (and no longer in relation to individual beings), as being in reality *Brahma* Itself, which is "without duality," and outside of which there is nothing, either manifested or unmanifested.[1] Besides, anything which leaves something outside itself cannot be infinite, being limited by that very thing which it excludes; and thus the World, taking this expression as meaning the whole of universal manifestation, is only distinguishable from *Brahma* in an illusory manner, whilst on the contrary *Brahma* is absolutely "distinct from that which It pervades,"[2] that is, from the World, since we cannot apply any of the determinative attributes to It which pertain to the World, and since universal manifestation in its entirety is rigorously nil in relation to Its Infinity.

As we have already pointed out elsewhere, this irreciprocity of relationship entails the formal condemnation of "pantheism," as well as of "immanentism" of any sort; and the *Bhagavadgītā* also asserts the same thing very clearly in the following terms: "All beings are in Me and I am not Myself in them.... My Being upholds beings and, without being Itself in them, it is through It that they exist."[3] Again, one may say that *Brahma* is the absolute Whole for the very reason that It is infinite, while, on the other hand, though all things are in *Brahma,* they are not *Brahma* when viewed from the standpoint of distinction, that is to say, in their quality of relative and conditioned things, their existence as such being, moreover, nothing but an illusion from the standpoint of supreme Reality. That which is asserted of things and which cannot apply to *Brahma* is but an expression of relativity, and at the same time, this relativity being illusory, all distinction is equally illusory, because one of its terms vanishes when brought into the presence of the other, nothing being capable of entering into correlation with the Infinite. It is solely in principle that all things are *Brahma,* but also it is that alone which constitutes their fundamental reality; this it is that must never be lost sight of if there is to be a proper understanding of what is to follow.[4]

"No distinction (bearing upon contingent modifications, such as the distinction between the agent, the act and the end or the result of that act) invalidates the essential unity and identity of *Brahma* as cause (*kārana*) and effect (*kārya*).[5] The sea is the same as its waters and does not differ (in nature) in any way from them, although the wages, the foam, the spray, the drops and other accidental modifications which these waters undergo exist apart or conjointly as different from one another (when considered distinctively, either under the aspect of succession or of simultaneity, but without their nature ceasing on that account to be the same).[6] An effect is not other (in essence) than its cause (although the cause, on the contrary, is more than the effect); *Brahma* is one (as Being) and without duality (as Supreme Principle); Itself, It is not separated (by any limitations) from Its modifications (formal as well as formless); It is *Ātmā* (in very possible state), and *Ātmā* (in itself, in the unconditioned state) is It (and not other than It).[7] The same earth yields diamonds and other precious minerals, crystal rocks and common worthless stones; the same soil produces a diversity of plants offering the greatest variety of leaves, flowers and fruits; the same nutriment is converted in the organism into blood, flesh and various excresences, such as hair and nails. As milk is spontaneously changed into curds and water into ice (but without this conversion from one state into another implying any change of nature), so *Brahma* modifies Itself in diverse ways (in the indefinite multiplicity of universal manifestation), without the aid of instruments or external means of any kind whatever (and without Its unity and identity being affected thereby, without it being possible to say, therefore, that It is modified in reality, although all things only exist in effect as Its modifications).[8] Thus the spider spins its web out of its own substance, subtle beings take diverse (incorporeal) forms, and the lotus grows from marsh to marsh without organs of locomotion. That *Brahma* is indivisible and without parts (as It is), is not objection (to this conception of universal multiplicity in Its unity, or rather in Its "non-duality"); it is not Its totality (eternally immutable) which is modified in the appearances of the World (nor any of Its parts, since It has none), but it is Itself viewed under the special aspect of distinction or of differentiation, that is, as *saguna* or *savishesha*: and, if It can be viewed thus, that is because It comprises all possibilities within Itself, without their being in any sense parts of Itself.[9] Divers changes (of condition and modes of existence) are presented to the same (individual) soul while dreaming (and in this state perceiving internal objects which belong to the domain of subtle manifestation);[10] divers illusory forms (corresponding to different modalities of formal manifestation, other than the corporeal modality) are assumed by this same subtle being without in any respect altering its unity (such illusory forms, *māyāvī-rūpa,* being considered as purely accidental and not belonging, of themselves, to the being who assumes them, so that the latter must be regarded as unaffected by this merely apparent modification).[11] *Brahma* is almighty (since It contains all things in principle), capable of every activity (although "actionless," or rather on that very account), without organ or instrument of action of any sort; therefore no motive or special end (such as pertains to an individual act) other than Its own will (which is indistinguishable from Its omnipotence),[12] must be assigned to the determination of the Universe. No accidental differentiation must be imputed to It (as in the case of a particular cause), because each individual being is modified (while developing its possibilities) in conformity with its own nature;[13] thus the rain-cloud distributes rain with impartiality (without regard to the special results which arise from secondary circumstances), and this same fertilising rain causes different seeds to grow in various ways, producing a variety of plants according to their species (by reason of the different potentialities proper to these seeds respectively).[14] Every attribute of a first cause is (in principle) in *Brahma,* which (in Itself) is nevertheless devoid of every (distinct) quality."[15]

"That which was, that which is and that which will be, truly all is *Omkāra* (the Universe principially identified with *Brahma,* and, as such, symbolized by the sacred monosyllable *Om*); and all else which is not subjected to threefold time (*trikāla,* that is the temporal condition viewed under its three modalities of past, present and future) is also truly *Omkāra.* Assuredly this *Ātmā* (of which all things are but the manifestation) is *Brahma,* and this *Ātmā* (relatively to the various states of the being) has four conditions (*pādas,* a word signifying literally "feet"); in truth, all this is *Brahma.*"[16]

"All this," (as moreover the continuation of this latter text, which we shall give later on, clearly shows), must be understood as referring to the different modalities of the individual being regarded in its integrality, as well as to the non-individual states of the total being; that is what is meant here by the conditions of *Ātmā* although, in itself, *Ātmā* is truly unconditioned and never ceases to be so.

REFERENCES

1. Mohyiddin ibn Arabi, in his *Treatise on Unity* (*Risālatul-Ahadiyah*), says in the same sense:

   "*Allah*—may He be exalted—is exempt from all comparison as well as from every rival, contrast or opposition." There is moreover perfect agreement in this respect also between the Vedānta and Moslem esoterism.
2. See the text of the treatise on the *Knowledge of the Self* (*Ātmā-bodha*) of Shankarāchārya, which will be quoted further on.
3. *Bhagavadgītā,* IX, 4 and 5.
4. We will here quote a Taoïst text in which the same ideas are expressed: "Do not inquire whether the Principle is in this or in that; It is in all beings. That is why It is given the epithet of great, supreme, entire, universal, total.... That which caused beings to be beings is not Itself subject to the same laws as beings. That which caused all beings to be limited, is Itself limitless, infinite.... As for manifestation, the Principle produces the succession of its phases, but is not that succession (nor involved in that succession). It is the author of causes and of effects (the prime cause), but is not the causes and effects (particular and manifested). It is the author of condensations and dissipations (births and deaths, changes of state), but is not Itself condensation or dissipation. Everything proceeds from It and is modified by and under Its influence. It is in all beings, by the determining of a norm; but It is not identical with beings, being neither differentiated nor limited." (*Chuang-tzu,* chap. XXII; French translation by Father Wieger, pp. 395-6).
5. It is as *Nirguna* that *Brahma* is *kārana,* and as *Saguna* that It is *kārya*; the former

is the "Supreme" or *Para Brahma* and the latter is the "Non-Supreme" or *Apara Brahma* (who is *Īshwara*); but it in no wise follows that *Brahma* ceases in any way to be "without duality" (*advaita*), for the "Non-Supreme" Itself is but illusory insofar as It is distinguished from the "Supreme", just as the effect is not truly and essentially different from the cause. It should be noted that *Para Brahma* and *Apara Brahma* ought never to be translated respectively as "superior *Brahma*" and "inferior *Brahma*", for such expressions presuppose a comparison or a correlation which cannot possibly exist.

6. This comparison with the sea and its waters shows that *Brahma* is here envisaged as Universal Possibility, which is the absolute totality of particular possibilities.
7. This is the very formula of the "Supreme Identity," in the most concise form that it is possible to give to it.
8. It must not be forgotten, in order to resolve this apparent difficulty, that we are here well beyond the distinction of *Purusha* and *Prakriti* and that both these two, being already unified in Being, are with all the more reason included in the supreme *Brahma,* and hence appear as two complementary aspects of the Principle, if one is permitted to use such an expression, for it is indeed relatively to our own conception only that they constitute two aspect: insofar as It is modified, that is the aspect analogues to *Prakriti;* insofar however as It is unmodified, that is the aspect analogous to *Purusha;* and it will be noticed that the latter answers more profoundly and more adequately than the former to the supreme reality in its changelessness. That is why *Brahma* Itself is *Purushottama* whereas *Prakriti* only represents, in relation to manifestation, Its *Shakti,* that is to say Its "productive will," which is properly speaking Its "Omnipotence" ("actionless" activity as regards the Principle, becoming passivity as regards the manifestation). It should be added that when this conception is thus transposed beyond Being, it is no longer with "Essence" and "Substance" that we are dealing, but rather with the Infinite and Possibility, as we hope to explain on another occasion; it is also what the Far Eastern tradition calls "Active Perfection" (*Khien*) and "Passive Perfection" (*Khouen*) which moreover coincide in Perfection in the absolute sense.
9. In Moslem esoterism also, Unity, considered insofar as it contains all the aspects of Divinity (*Asrār Rabbāniyah* or the "Dominical mysteries"), "is the reverberating surface of the Absolute with its innumerable facets which magnifies every creature that is mirrored directly in it." This surface is likewise *Māyā* taken in its highest sense, as the *Shakti* of *Brahma,* that is to say the "Omnipotence" of the Supreme Principle. Again in an exactly similar way, in the Jewish *Qabbalah, Kether* (the first of the ten *Sephiroth*) is the "garment" of *Aīn-Soph* (the Infinite or the Absolute).
10. The modifications produced in a dream offer one of the most striking analogies that it is possible to put forward in illustration of the multiplicity of the states of the being; we shall therefore have occasion to speak of it again if, as we intend, we one day set forth this metaphysical theory more completely.
    [M. Guénon carried out this project in *Les États Multiplès de L'Être,* which is to be published in the present series of translation,—Translator.]
11. In connection with this point an interesting comparison can be made with the teaching of Catholic theologians, and especially of St. Thomas Aquinas, on the subject of the forms that angels are able to assume; the similarity is all the more

remarkable in that the points of view are naturally very different. We will likewise recall in passing what we have already had occasion to point out elsewhere, namely that almost everything that is said theologically of the angels can also be said metaphysically of the higher states of the being.

12. It is Its *Shakti* which we have spoken of in previous footnotes, and it is also itself insofar as It is considered as Universal Possibility; moreover, in itself, the *Shakti* can only be an aspect of the Principle, and if it is distinguished from the Principle in order to be "separatively" considered, it is then nothing but the "Great Illusion" (*Mahā-moha*), that is to say *Māyā* in its inferior and exclusively cosmic sense.
13. This is precisely the idea of *Dharma,* conceived as "conformity to the essential nature of beings," applied to the entire order of universal Existence.
14. "O Principle! Thou who bestowest on all beings that which befits them, Thou hast never claimed to be called equitable. Thou whose benefits extend to all times, Thou hast never claimed to be called charitable. Thou who wast before the beginning, and who dost not claim to be called venerable; Thou who enfoldest and supportest the Universe, producing all its forms, without claiming to be called skilful; it is in Thee that I move." (*Chuang-tzu,* chap. VI; Father Wieger's French translation, p. 261.)

    "It can be said of the Principle only that It is the origin of everything and that It influences all while remaining indifferent." (Ibid., chap. XXII, p. 391.)

    "The Principle, indifferent, impartial, lets all things follow their course without influencing them. It claims no title (no qualification or attribution whatsoever). It acts not. Doing nothing, there is nothing It does not do." (Ibid., chap. XXV, p. 437.)
15. *Brahma-sūtras,* Adhyāya II, Pāda I, sūtras 13-37. Cp. *Bhagavadgītā,* IX, 4-8: "It is I, devoid of every sensible form, who have developed all this Universe.... Immutable in my productive power (*Shakti,* who here is called *Prakriti* because it is considered in relation to manifestation), I produce and reproduce (throughout all the cycles) the multitude of beings, without a determinate aim, and by the sole virtue of that productive power."
16. *Māndukya Upanishad,* shrutis 1 and 2.

CHAPTER 11

The Different Conditions of Ātmā in the Human Being

We will now enter upon a more detailed study of the different conditions of the individual being, residing in the living form, which, as previously explained, includes the subtle form (*sūkshma-sharīra* or *linga-sharīra*) on the one hand and the gross or bodily form (*sthūla-sharīra*) on the other. The conditions we are referring to must not be confused with that particular condition which we have already noted as being special to each individual, distinguishing him from all other individuals, nor are they connected with that aggregate of limiting conditions defining each state of existence taken separately; in this instance we are referring exclusively to the various states or, if it be preferred, the various modalities to which, in a perfectly general way, any single individual being is subject, whatever the nature of that being may be. These modalities taken as a whole, can always be related both to the gross and to the subtle state, the former being confined to the bodily modality and the latter comprising the remainder of the individuality (there is no question here of the other individual states, since it is the human state in particular that we are considering). What is beyond these two states no longer belongs to the individual as such; we are referring to what may be called the "causal" state, that is to say the state which corresponds to *kārana-sharīra* and which belongs consequently to the universal and formless order. With this causal state moreover, though we are no longer in the realm of individual existence, we are still in the realm of Being; therefore, it is necessary in addition to envisage, beyond Being, a fourth, absolutely unconditioned, principial state. Metaphysically all these states, even those which belong strictly to the individual, are related to *Ātmā,* that is to say to the Personality, since it is this alone which constitutes the fundamental reality of the being and since every state of that being would be purely illusory if one attempted to separate it from *Ātmā*. The being's different states, whatever their nature, represent nothing but possibilities of *Ātmā*; that is why it is possible to speak of the various conditions in which the being finds itself as in the truest sense conditions of *Ātmā,* although it must be clearly understood that *Ātmā,* in itself, is in no way affected thereby and does not on that account cease to be unconditioned, in the same way that it never becomes manifested, although it is the essential and transcendent principle of manifestation in all its modes.

Disregarding for the moment the fourth state, to which we shall return later, the first three states are: the waking state, corresponding to gross manifestation; the dream state, corresponding to subtle manifestation; and deep sleep, which is the "causal" and formless state. Besides these three states another is sometimes mentioned, that of death, and even a further one, the state of ecstatic trance, considered as intermediate (*sandhyā*)[1] between deep sleep and death, in the same way that dreaming is intermediate between waking and deep sleep.[2] These two last states however are not generally reckoned as separate since they are not essentially distinct from that of deep sleep, which is really an extra-individual state, as we have just explained, and in which the being returns likewise into non-manifestation, or at least into the formless, "the living soul (*jīvātmā*) withdrawing into the bosom of the Universal Spirit (*Ātmā*) along the path which leads to the very centre of the being, where is the seat of *Brahma.*"[3]

For the detailed description of these states we have only to turn to the text of the *Māndūkya Upanishad,* the opening passage of which we have already cited with the exception of one phrase, however, the first of all, which runs: "*Om,* this syllable (*akshara*)[4] is everything that is: its explanation follows." The sacred monosyllable *Om,* which expresses the essence of the Veda,[5] is here taken as the ideographic symbol of *Ātmā*. This syllable, composed of three letters (*mātrās,* these letters being *a, u* and *m,* the first two contracting into *o*),[6] has four elements, the fourth of which, being none other than the monosyllable itself regarded synthetically under its principial aspect, is "non-expressed" by any latter (*amātra*), being prior to all distinction in the "indissoluble" (*akshara*); similarly *Ātmā* has four conditions (*pādas*), the fourth of which is not really a special condition at all but is *Ātmā* regarded in Itself, in an absolutely transcendent manner independently of any condition and which, as such, is not susceptible of any representation. We will now go on to explain what the text we referred to says on the subject of each of these conditions of *Ātmā*, starting from the last degree, that of manifestation, and working back to the supreme, total and unconditioned state.

References

1. The word *sandhyā* (derived from *sandhi,* the point of contact or of junction between two things) is also used, in a more ordinary sense, to describe the twilight (morning and evening) similarly considered as intermediate between day and night; in the theory of cosmic cycles it indicates the interval between two *yugas.*
2. Concerning this state cp. *Brahma-sūtras,* Adhyāya III, Pāda 2, sūtra 10.
3. *Brahma-sūtra,* Adhyāya III, Pāda 2, sūtras 7 and 8.
4. The word *akshara* etymologically means "indissoluble" or "indestructible"; if the syllable is referred to by means of this word, this is because the syllable (and not the alphabetical letter) is looked upon as constituting the primitive unit and fundamental element of language; moreover every verbal root is syllabic. A verbal root in Sanskrit is called *dhātu,* a word properly meaning "seed", because, through the possibilities of multiple modification that it carries and contains in itself, it is indeed the seed which, by its development, gives birth to the entire language. It may be said that the root is the fixed and invariable element in a word, representing its fundamental and immutable nature, to which secondary and variable elements come to be added, representing accidents (in the etymological sense) or modifications of the principal idea.
5. Cp. *Chhāndogya Upanishad,* Prapāthaka I, Khanda 1 and Prapāthaka II, Khanda 23; also *Brihadāranyaka Upanishad,* Adhyāya V, Brāhmana 1, shruti 1.
6. In Sanskrit the vowel *o* is actually formed from the combination of *a* and *u,* just as the vowel *e* is formed from the union of *a* and *i.* Likewise in Arabic, the three vowels *a, i,* and *u* are the only ones that are considered fundamental and really distinct.

Chapter 12

The Waking State or the Condition of Vaishwānara

The first condition is *Vaishwānara,* the seat[1] of which is in the waking state (*jāgaritasthāna*), which has knowledge of external (sensible) objects, which has seven members and nineteen mouths and the world of gross manifestation for its province.[2]

Vaishwānara, as the etymological derivation of the word indicates,[3] is what we have called "Universal Man," regarded however more especially in the complete development of his states of manifestation and under the particular aspect of that development. Here the extent of this term appears to be limited to one of these states only, the most external of all, that of gross manifestation, which constitutes the corporeal world; but this particular state can be taken as the symbol for the whole of universal Manifestation, of which it is an element, since for the human being it is necessarily the basis and point of departure for all realization; as in all symbolism therefore, it will suffice to effect the transposition appropriate to the degree to which the conception is called upon to apply. It is in this sense that the state in question can be related to "Universal Man" and described as constituting his body, conceived by analogy with the body of individual man, an analogy which is that of the macrocosm (*ādhidevaka*) and the microcosm (*ādhyātmika*), as we have already explained. Under this aspect *Vaishwānara* is also identified with *Virāj,* that is to say with the cosmic Intelligence insofar as it governs and unifies in its integrality the whole of the corporeal world. Finally, from another point of view, which however corroborates the preceding one, *Vaishwānara* also means "that which is common to all men"; in that case it is the human species, understood as specific nature, or more exactly what may be called "the genius of the species."[4] Furthermore it should be observed that the corporeal state is in fact common to all human individuals whatever may be the other modalities in which they are capable of developing themselves in order to realize, as individuals and without going beyond the the human level,[5] the full range of their respective possibilities.

After what has just been said it will be easy for us to explain the significance of the seven members mentioned in the *Māndūkya Upanishad* and which form the seven principal parts of the macrocosmic body of *Vaishwānara.* Taking them in order: (1) the assemblage of the higher luminous spheres, that is to say of the higher states of being (considered however in this instance solely in their relationship with the particular state in question), is compared with the part of the head containing the brain, for the brain in fact corresponds organically with the "mental" function, which is but a reflection of the intelligible Light or of the supra-individual principles; (2) the sun and the moon, or more exactly the principles represented in the sensible world by these two luminaries[6] are the two eyes; (3) the igneous principle is the mouth;[7] (4) the directions of space (*dish*) are the ears;[8] (5) the atmosphere, that is to say the cosmic environment whence the "vital breath" (*prāna*) proceeds, corresponds to the lungs; (6) the intermediate region (*Antariksha*), extending between the Earth (*Bhū* or *Bhūmi*) and the luminous spheres or the Heavens (*Swar* or *Swarga*) and considered as the region where forms (still potential in relation to the gross state) are elaborated, corresponds to the stomach;[9] (7) finally the Earth, that is to say, symbolically, the final term in actuation of the entire corporeal manifestation, corresponds to the feet, which are taken here as the emblem of the whole lower portion of the body. The relationship of these various members to one another and their functions in the cosmic whole to which they belong is analogous (but not identical, be it understood) with the relationship between the corresponding part of the human organism. It will be noticed that no mentioned is made here of the heart, because its direct relationship with universal Intelligence places it outside the sphere of the individual functions properly so called, and because this "seat of *Brahma*" is really and truly the central point both in the cosmic and in the human orders, whereas everything pertaining to manifestation, and above all to formal manifestation is external and "peripheric," if one may so express it, belonging exclusively to the circumference of the "wheel of things."

In the condition we are describing, *Ātmā,* as *Vaishwānara,* becomes conscious of the world of sensible manifestation (considered also as the sphere of that aspect of "non-supreme" *Brahma* which is called *Virāj*). It does so by means of nineteen organs, which are described as so many mouths, because they are the "entrance-ways" of knowledge for everything belonging to this particular domain; moreover the intellectual assimilation which operates in knowledge is often compared symbolically with the vital assimilation effected by nutrition. These nineteen organs (also including in that term the corresponding faculties, in accordance with our previous explanation of the general significance of the word *indriya*) are: the five organs of sensation, the five organs of action, the five vital breaths (*vāyus*), the "mental" faculty or the inward sense (*manas*), the intellect (*buddhi,* considered here exclusively in its relation to the individual state), thought (*chitta*), conceived as the faculty which gives for to ideas and which associates them one with another, and finally individual consciousness (*ahankāra*): these are the faculties which we have already studied in detail. Each organ and each faculty of every individual belonging to the domain in question, that is to say to the corporeal world, proceeds respectively from it corresponding organ or faculty in *Vaishwānara;* of this organ and faculty it is in a certain sense one of the constitute elements, in the same way that the individual to which it belongs is an element of the cosmic whole, in which, for its part and in the place allotted to it (form the fact that it is that individual being and not another), it contributes of necessity towards making up the total harmony.[10]

The waking state, in which the activity of the organs and faculties in question of exercised, is described as the first of the conditions of *Ātmā,* although the gross or corporeal modality to which it corresponds occupies the lowest degree in the order of development (*prapancha*) of manifestation, starting from its primordial and unmanifested principle; it marks indeed the limit of that development, at least in relation to the state of existence in which human individuality is situated. The reason for this apparent anomaly has already been explained: it is in this corporeal modality that we find the basis and point of departure, firstly of individual realization (that is to say of the full realization of the individuality in its integral extension), and afterwards of all further realization which lies beyond the individual possibilities and implies the taking possession by the being of its higher states. Consequently if, instead of placing oneself at the point of view of the development of manifestation, one places oneself, as we are doing at present, at the point of view of the this realization with its various degrees, the order of which necessarily proceeds in the contrary direction, from the manifested to the unmanifested, then in that case of waking state must clearly be looked upon as in fact preceding the states of dreaming and deep sleep, which correspond respectively to the extra-corporeal modalities of the individuality and to the supra-individual states of the being.

References

1. It is obvious that this and all similar expressions such as abode, residence, etc., must always be understood in this context symbolically and not literally, that is to say they must be taken as indicating not a place but rather a modality of existence. The use of a spatial symbolism is moreover extremely widespread, a fact which can be accounted for by the actual nature of the conditions governing corporeal individuality, and which dictate the terms in which any translation of the truths that concern other states of the being must necessarily be expressed, insofar as such expression is possible. The term *sthāna* has as its exact equivalent and word "state" (*status*), for the root *sthā* reappears in the Latin *stare* and its derivatives, with the same meanings as in Sanskrit.
2. *Māndūkya Upanishad,* shruti 3.
3. On this derivation, see Shankarāchārya's commentary on the *Brahma-sūtras,* Adhyāya I, Pāda 2, sūtra 28: it is *Ātmā* who is both "all" (*vishwa*) when He appears as the Personality, and "man" (*nara*) when he appears as the individuality (that is to say as *jīvātmā*). *Vaishwānara* is therefore a title which is properly befitting to *Ātmā*; on the other hand it is also a name of *Agni,* as we shall see further on (cp. *Shatapatha Brāhmana*).
4. In this connection *nara* or *nri* is man considered as an individual belonging to the human species, whereas *mānava* is more exactly man in his capacity as a thinking being, that is to say as a being endowed with the mental faculty, which is moreover the essential attribute inherent in his species and the one by which the nature of this species is characterised. On the other hand, the name *nara* is none the less capable of being transposed analogically so as to be identified with *Purusha*; and thus it comes about that Vishnu is sometimes referred to as *Narottama* or "Supreme Man," a name which must not be taken as implying the least trace of anthropomorphism, any more than the conception of "Universal Man" under all its aspects; and this is true precisely in virtue of this transposition. We cannot here undertake an investigation of the manifold and complex meanings implied in the word *nara;* as for the nature of the species, a whole special study would be needed to deal adequately with the developments to which it may give rise.
5. It would be illuminating to establish points of concordance with the conception of "adamic" nature in the Jewish and Moslem traditions, a conception which likewise is applicable at different levels and in senses hierarchically superposed;

but this would lead us too far afield and at the moment we must limit ourselves to this bare reference.

6. Here one might recall the symbolical meanings which the Sun and Moon bear in the Western Hermetic tradition and in the cosmological theories that the Alchemists based on it; in neither case must the designation of these heavenly bodies be taken literally. It should also be observed that the present symbolism differs from that previously alluded to, according to which the Sun and the Moon correspond respectively to the heart and the brain; here again long explanations would be necessary in order to show how these different points of view are reconciled and harmonised in the whole framework of analogical correspondences.
7. We have already mentioned that *Vaishwānara* is occasionally a name of *Agni,* who is then chiefly considered in the guise of animating warmth, therefore in the form in which he is dwelling in living things; we shall have occasion to refer to this again at a later stage. Furthermore, *mukhya-prāna* is both the breath of the moth (*mūkha*) and the principal vital act (it is in the latter sense that the five *vāyus* are its modalities); and warmth is intimately associated with life itself.
8. One may notice the remarkable relationship between this symbolism and the physiological function of the semi-circular canals.
9. In one sense, the word *Antariksha* also includes the atmosphere, which is then considered as the medium of diffusion of light; it is also worth nothing that the agent of that diffusion is not Air (*Vāyu*) but Ether (*Ākāsha*). When the terms are transposed in order to make them applicable to the entirely of the states of universal manifestation, *Antariksha* is identified with *Bhuvas,* the middle term of the *Tribhuvana,* which is ordinarily described as the atmosphere, the word being taken however in a much more extended and less determinate sense than in the preceding case. The names of the three worlds, *Bhū, Bhuvas* and *Svar,* are the three *vyāhritis,* words which are usually uttered after the monosyllable *Om* in the Hindu rites of *Sandhyā-upāsanā* (a meditation repeated in the morning, at mid-day and in the evening). It is noticeable that the first two of the three names derive from the same root, because they refer to modalities of the same state of existence, namely that of human individuality, while the third represents, in this division, the whole of the higher states.
10. This harmony is also an aspect of *Dharma:* it is the equilibrium in which all disequilibriums are compensated, the order which is made up of the sum of all partial and apparent disorders.

Chapter 13

The Dream State or the Condition of Taijasa

The second condition is *Taijasa* (the "Luminous," a word derived from *tejas,* the igneous element), whose seat is in the dream state (*swapna-sthāna*), which has knowledge of inward (mental) objects, which has seven members and nineteen mouths and whose domain is the world of subtle manifestation."[1]

In this state the outward faculties, whilst existing all the time potentially, are reabsorbed into the inward sense (*manas*), which is at the same time their common source, their support and their immediate end, and which resides in the luminous arteries (*nādīs*) of the subtle form, where it is distributed without any division of its nature in the manner of a diffused heat. The igneous element, in itself, considered in its essential properties, is indeed at one and the same time light and heat; and, as the very name *Taijasa* applied to the subtle state indicates, these two aspects, suitably transposed (since there is no longer any question here of sensible qualities) must be found in that state also. As we have already had occasion to remark elsewhere, everything belonging to the subtle state is very closely connected with the nature of life itself, which is inseparable from heat; and it may be recalled that on this point, as on many others, the conceptions of Aristotle are in complete agreement with those of the East. As to the luminosity to which we have just alluded, it should be regarded as the reflection and diffraction of the intelligible Light in the extra-sensible modalities of formal manifestation (among which however it is only necessary in the present instance to consider those relating to the human state). Furthermore, the subtle form itself (*sūkshma-sharīra* or *linga-sharīra*) in which *Taijasa* dwells is likened to a fiery vehicle,[2] although this must of course be distinguished from corporeal fire (the element *tejas* or that which derives from it) which is perceived by the senses of the gross form (*sthūla-sharīra*), vehicle of *Vaishwānara,* and more particularly by sight, since visibility, necessarily presupposing the presence of light, is the sensible quality naturally belonging to *tejas*; in the subtle state however there can no longer be any question of *bhūtas,* but only of the corresponding *tanmātras* which are their immediate determining principles.

As to the *nādīs* or arteries belonging to the subtle form, they should on no account be confused with the corporeal arteries by means of which the circulation of the blood is effected; physiologically, they correspond rather to the ramifications of the nervous system, for they are expressly described as luminous; morever, just as fire is in a sense polarized into heat and light, so the subtle state is linked to the corporeal state in two different and complementary ways, through, the blood as to the caloric and through the nervous system as to the luminous quality.[3] At the same time it must be clearly understood that between the *nādīs* and the nerves there is correspondence only and not identification, since the former are not corporeal and we are really concerned with two different spheres within the integral individuality. Similarly, when a relationship is established between the functions of these *nādīs* and respiration,[4] because respiration is essential for maintaining life and corresponds in a real way to the principal vital act, it should not be concluded on that account that they can be represented as canals of some sort in which the air circulates; this would amount to confusing the "vital breath" (*prāna*), which properly belongs to the order of subtle manifestation, with a bodily function.[5] It is said that the total number of *nādīs* is seventy-two thousand; according to other texts however it would appear to be seven hundred and twenty millions; but the difference here is more apparent than real, since these numbers are meant to be taken symbolically and not literally, as is usual in such cases; and this will be apparent if one observes their obvious connection with the cyclic numbers.[6] Further on we shall have occasion to supplement our remarks upon the subject of the subtle arteries as well as on the different stages in the process of reabsorption of the individual faculties: as we have said, this reabsorption is effected in an order inverse to the development of those same faculties.

In the dream state the individual "living soul" (*jīvātmā*) "is to itself its own light" and it produces, through the action of its own desire (*kāma*) alone, a world issuing entirely from itself, in which the objects consist exclusively of mental conceptions, that is to say of combinations of ideas clothed in subtle forms, depending substantially upon the subtle form of the individual himself, of which they are merely so many secondary and accidental modifications.[7]

There is however always something incomplete and uncoordinated about this production: it is for this reason that it is looked upon as illusory (*māyāmaya*) or as only possessing an apparent (*prātibhāsika*) existence whereas, in the sensible world where it is situated in the waking state, the same "living soul" possesses the faculty of acting in the sense of a practical (*vyāvahārika*) production, also illusory no doubt with regard to absolute (*paramārtha*) reality and transitory like all manifestation, yet nevertheless possessing a relative reality and a stability sufficient for the needs of ordinary "profane" life (*laukika,* a word derived from *loka,* the "world," which should here be taken in a sense exactly equivalent to that which it normally bears in the Gospels). However it is important to observe that this difference respecting the orientation of the activity of the being in the two states does not imply an effective superiority of the waking state over the dream state when each is considered in itself; at least a superiority which is valid only from a "profane" point of view cannot metaphysically be considered as a real superiority; and indeed from another point of view the possibilities of the dream state are more extensive than those of the waking state and they allow the individual to escape in a certain measure from some of the limiting conditions to which he is subject in the corporeal modality.[8] But, however that may be, the absolutely real (*pāramārthika*) is the Self (*Ātmā*) alone; it is utterly unattainable by any conception that confines itself to the consideration of external and internal objects, knowledge of which constitutes respectively the waking and dream states; certain heterodox schools, which did in fact restrict their attention in this way to the aggregate of these two states, thereby condemned themselves to remain wholly enclosed within the limits of formal manifestation and the human individuality.

By reason of its connection with the mental faculty the realm of subtle manifestation can be described as an ideal world, to distinguish it form the sensible world which is the realm of gross manifestation. This term however should not be taken in the sense of Plato's "intelligible world," since his "ideas" are possibilities in the principial state, which must be referred to formless being (in spite of the over-imaginative expressions in which Plato often enveloped his thoughts): in the subtle state we are still only concerned with ideas clothed in forms, since the possibilities which this state comprises do not extend beyond individual existence.[9] Above all it is important not to be misled into imagining an opposition here of the kind which certain modern philosophers claim to establish between "ideal" and "real"; such an opposition is really quite meaningless. Everything that is, under whatever mode it may happen to exist, is real for that very reason and possesses precisely the type and degree of reality consonant with its own nature: something consisting in ideas (and that is all the meaning properly attributable to the word "ideal") is neither more nor less real on that account than something consisting in anything else, each possibility necessarily finding its position at that level in the universal hierarchy determined for it by its own nature.

In the order of universal manifestation, just as the sensible world, in its entirety, is identified with *Virāj,* so this ideal world of which we have been speaking is identified with *Hiranyagarbha* (literally, the "Golden Embryo"),[10] which is Brahmā (determination of *Brahma* as effect, *kārya*)[11] enveloping Himself in the "World Egg" (*Brahmānda*),[12] out of which there will develop, according to its mode of realization, the whole formal manifestation which is contained therein virtually as a conception of this *Hiranyagarbha,* primordial germ of the cosmic Light.[13] Furthermore *Hiranyagarbha* is described as the "synthetic aggregate of life" (*jīva-ghana*);[14] indeed it can really be identified with "Universal Life,"[15] by reason of the previously mentioned connection between the subtle state and life, which, even when considered in its entire extension (and not limited to organic or corporeal life only, to which field the physiological point of view is restricted),[16] is nevertheless but one of the special conditions of the state of existence to which human individuality belongs. The sphere of life therefore does not extend beyond the possibilities comprised within that state, which, be it understood, should here be viewed integrally and taken as including the subtle modalities as well as the gross modality.

Whether one places oneself at the "macrocosmic" point of view, as we have just done, or at the "microcosmic" point of view which we adopted to begin with, the ideal world in question is conceived by faculties corresponding analogically to those by which the sensible world is perceived, or if it be preferred, which are the same faculties as these in principle (since they are still individual faculties), but considered under another mode of existence and at another degree of development, their activity being exercised in a different realm. This explains how *Ātmā* in this dream state, that is to say under the aspect of *Taijasa,* comes to have the same number of members and mouth (or instruments of knowledge) as in the waking state under the aspect of *Vaishwānara.*[17]

There is no necessity to enumerate them a second time since the definitions we have already given can be applied equally, by means of a suitable transposition, to the two realms of gross or sensible manifestation and subtle or ideal manifestation.

References

1. *Māndūkya Upanishad,* shruti 4. In this text the subtle state is called *pravivikta,* literally "predistinguished," because it is a state of distinction that precedes gross manifestation; the word also means "separate," because the "living soul," when in the dream-state, is to all intents confined within itself, contrary to what happens in the waking state which is "common to all men."
2. Elsewhere in the connection we have recalled the "chariot of fire" upon which the prophet Elijah was taken up to heaven (II Kings, ii.11).
3. We have already mentioned, in describing the constitution of the *annamaya-kosha,* which is the bodily organism, that the elements of the nervous system originate from the assimilation of fiery substances. As for blood, being liquid, it is formed originally from watery substances, but these must have undergone an elaboration due to the action of the vital heat, which is the manifestation of *Agni Vaishwānara,* and they only play the part of a plastic support that serves for the fixation of an element of igneous nature: fire and water here represent, in relation to one another, "essence" and "substance" in a relative sense. One might easily compare this with certain alchemical theories, such as those which introduce the principles called "sulphur" and "mercury", the one active and the other passive, which are respectively analogous, in the order of "mixed things," to fire and water in the order of elements; not to mention the many other designations that are conferred symbolically, in the Hermetic language, on the two correlative terms of a duality of this nature.
4. We are alluding here more especially to the teachings connected with *Hatha-yoga,* that is to say to the methods preparatory to "Union" (*yoga* in the proper sense of the word), which are based on the assimilation of certain rhythms, chiefly bound up with breath-control. What the Islamic esoteric schools call *dhikr* fulfils exactly the same function, and often indeed the actual proceedings resorted to are quite similar in both traditions, a fact however which is not to be taken as evidence of any borrowing; the science or rhythm, in fact, may well be known in two different quarters quite independently, for we are dealing here with a science having its own definite object and corresponding to a clearly

defined order of reality, although this science is quite unknown to Westerners.

5. This confusion has actually been perpetrated by certain orientalists, whose understanding is doubtless unable to operate outside the limits of the corporeal world.
6. The fundamental cyclic numbers are: $72 = 2^3 \times 3^2$; $108 = 2^2 \times 3^3$; $432 = 2^4 \times 3^3 = 72 \times 6 = 108 \times 4$; they apply for example to the geometrical division of a circle ($360 = 72 \times 5 = 12 \times 30$) and to the duration of the astronomical period of the precession of the equinoxes ($72 \times 360 = 432 \times 60 = 25{,}920$ years). These are this most immediate and elementary applications, but we cannot enter now into the properly symbolical considerations that arise out of the transposition of these data into different orders.
7. Cp. *Brihadāranyaka Upanishad,* Adhyāya IV, Brāhmana 3, shrutis 9 and 10.
8. On the dream state cp. *Brahma-sūtras,* Adhyāya IV, Pāda 2, sūtras 1-6.
9. The subtle state is properly the realm of ψυχη and not that of νους; the latter in reality corresponds to *buddhi,* that is to say to the supra-individual intellect.
10. This name bears a meaning very close to that of *Taijasa,* for gold, according to the Hindu doctrine, is the "mineral light"; the alchemists also looked on it as corresponding by analogy, among the metals, to the sun among the planets; and it is at least a remarkable fact that the Latin name for gold itself (*anrum*) is striking similar to the Hebrew *aor,* which means "light".
11. It must be pointed out hat Brahmā is a masculine form, while *Brahma* is neuter; that indispensable distinction, which is of the highest importance (since it expresses the distinction of the "Supreme" from the "non-Supreme") cannot be indicated if, as is usual among orientalists, one employs the single form of *Brahman* which belongs to either gender; the latter practice leads to perpetual confusion, especially in a language like French where the neuter gender is wanting.
12. This cosmogonic symbol of the "World-Egg" is in no wise peculiar to India; it is for example to be found in Mazdeism, in the Egyptian tradition (the Egg of *Kneph*), in that of the Druids and in the Orphic tradition. The embryonic condition which in each individual being plays a corresponding part to that played by *Brahmānda* in the cosmic order, is in Sanskrit called *pinda*; and the analogy between the "microcosm" and the "macrocosm", considered under this aspect, is expressed in the following formula: *Yathā pinda tathā Brahmānda,* "as the individual embryo, so the World-Egg."
13. That is why *Virāj* proceeds from *Hiranyagarbha,* and *Manu,* in turn. Proceeds from *Virāj.*
14. The word *ghana* signifies primarily a cloud, and thence a compact and undifferentiated mass.
15. "And the life was the light of men" (*St. John,* I.4).
16. We are especially alluding to the extension of the idea of life which is implied in the point of view of the Western religions, and which in fact relates to possibilities contained in a prolongation of human individuality; as we have explained elsewhere, this is what the Far-Eastern tradition refers to under the name of "longevity."
17. These faculties must here be regarded as distributed in the three "envelopes," which by their combination constitute the subtle form (*vijnānamaya-kosha, manomaya-kosha* and *prānamaya-kosha*).

Chapter 14

The State of Deep Sleep or the Condition of Prājna

"When the being who is asleep experiences no desire and is not the subject of any dream, his state is that of deep sleep (*sushupta-sthāna*): he (that is to say *Ātmā* itself in this condition) who in this state has become one (without any distinction or differentiation),[1] who has identified himself with a synthetic whole (unique and without particular determination) or integral Knowledge (*Prajnāna-ghana*),[2] who is filled (by inmost penetration and assimilation) with Beatitude (*ānandamaya*), actually enjoying that Beatitude (*ānanda*, as his own realm) and whose mouth (the instrument of knowledge) is (exclusively) total Consciousness (*chit*) itself (without intermediary or particularisation of any sort), that one is called *Prājna* (He who knows above and beyond any special condition): this is the third condition."[3]

As will at once be apparent, the vehicle of *Ātmā* in this state is the *kārana-sharīra,* since this is *ānandamaya-kosha*: and although it is spoken of analogically as a vehicle or an envelope, it is not really something distinct from *Ātmā* itself, since here we are beyond the sphere of distinction. Beatitude is made up of all the possibilities of *Ātmā*: it is, one might say, the sum itself of these possibilities: and if *Ātmā,* as *Prājna,* enjoys this Beatitude as its rightful kingdom, that is because it is really nothing else than the plenitude of its being, as we have already pointed out. This is essentially a formless and supra-individual state; it cannot therefore have anything to do with a "psychic" or "psychological" state, as certain orientalists have supposed . The psychic properly speaking is in fact the subtle state; and in making this assimilation we take the word "psychic" in its primitive sense, as used by the ancients, without concerning ourselves with the various far more specialized meanings which have been attached to it in later times, whereby it cannot be made to apply even to the whole of the subtle state. As for modern Western psychology, it deals only with quite a restricted portion of the human individuality, where the mental faculty is in direct relationship with the corporeal modality, and, given the methods it employs, it is incapable of going any further. In any case the very objective which it sets before itself and which is exclusively the study of mental phenomena, limits it strictly to the realm of the individuality, so that the state which we are now discussing necessarily eludes its investigations. Indeed it might even be said that that state is doubly inaccessible to it, in the first place because it lies beyond the mental sphere or the sphere of discursive and differentiated thought, and in the second place because it lies equally beyond all phenomena of any kind, that is to say beyond all formal manifestation.

This state of undifferentiation, in which all knowledge, including that of the other states, is synthetically centralized in the essential and fundamental unity of the being, is the unmanifested and "non-developed" (*avyakta*) state, principle and cause (*kārana*) of all manifestation and the source from which manifestation, is developed in the multiplicity of its different states and more particularly, as concerns the human being, in its subtle and gross states. This unmanifested state, conceived as root of the manifested (*vyakta*), which is only its effect (*kārya*), is identified in this respect with *Mūla Prakriti,* "Primordial Nature": but in reality it is *Purusha* as well as *Prakriti,* containing them both in its own undifferentiation, for it is cause in the complete sense of the word, that is to say both at one and the same time "efficient cause" and "material cause", to use the ordinary terminology, to which however we much prefer the expressions "essential cause" and "substantial cause", since these two complementary aspects of causality do in fact relate respectively to "essence" and to "substance", in the sense we have previously given to those words. If *Ātmā,* in this third state, is thus beyond the distinction of *Purusha* and *Prakriti,* or of the two poles of manifestation, that is simply because it is no longer situated within conditioned existence, but actually at the level of pure Being; nevertheless *Purusha* and *Prakriti,* which are themselves still unmanifested, should be included within it and this is even in a sense true, as we shall see later on, of the formless states of manifestation as well, which it has already been necessary to attach to the Universal, since they are really supra-individual states of the being; moreover it has to be remembered that all manifested states are contained, synthetically and in principle, within unmanifestated Being.

In this state the different objects of manifestation, including those of individual manifestation, external as well as internal, are not destroyed, but subsist in principial mode, being unified by the very fact that they are no longer conceived under the secondary or contingent aspect of distinction; of necessity they find themselves among the possibilities of the Self and the latter remains conscious in itself of all these possibilities, as "non-distinctively" beheld in integral Knowledge, from the very fact of being conscious of its own permanence in the "eternal present."[4] Were it otherwise and were the objects of manifestation not thus to subsist principially (a supposition impossible in itself, however, because these objects would then be but a pure nothing, which could not exist at all, not even in illusory mode) there could be no return from the state of deep sleep to the states of dreaming and waking, since all formal manifestation would be irremediably destroyed for the being once it had entered deep sleep; but in fact take place, at least for the being who is not actually "delivered," that is to say definitely freed from the conditions of individual existence.

The term *chit,* unlike its previous mentioned derivative *chitta,* must not be understood in the restricted sense of individual and formal thought (this restrictive determination, which implies a modification by reflection, being marked in the derivative by the suffix *kta,* which is the termination of the passive participle) but in the universal sense, as the total Consciousness of the "Self" looked at in its relationship with its unique object, which is *ānanda* or Beatitude.[5] This object, while constituting in a certain sense an envelope of the "Self" (*ānandamaya-kosha*), as we have already explained, is identical with the subject itself, which is *Sat* or pure Being and is not really distinct from it, as indeed it could not be, once there is no longer any real distinction.[6] Thus these three, *Sat, Chit* and *Ānanda* (generally united as *Sachchidānanda*)[7] are but one single and identical entity, and this "one" is *Ātmā,* considered outside and beyond all the particular conditions which determine each of its various states of manifestation.

In this state, which is also sometimes called by the name of *samprasāda* or "serenity,"[8] the intelligible Light is seized directly, that is to say by intellectual intuition, and no longer by reflection through the mental faculty (*manas*) as occurs in the individual states. We have previously applied this expression "intellectual intuition" to *buddhi,* faculty of supra-rational and supra-individual knowledge, although already manifested: in this respect therefore *buddhi* must in a way be included in the state of *Prājna,* which thus will comprise everything which is beyond individual existence. We have therefore to consider a new ternary group in Being constituted by *Purusha, Prakriti* and *Buddhi,* that is to say by the two poles of manifestation, "essence" and "substance," and by the first production of *Prakriti* under the influence of *Purusha,* this production being formless manifestation. Moreover it must be added that this ternary group only represents what might be called the "outwardness" of Being and does not therefore coincide in any way with the other principial group we have just described and which refers really to its "inwardness"; it would amount rather to a first particularisation of Being in distinctive mode.[9] It goes without saying of course that in speaking here of outward and inward, we are using a purely analogical language, based upon a spatial symbolism and which could not apply literally to pure Being. Furthermore the ternary group *Sachchidānanda,* which is co-extensive with Being, is transposed again, in the order of formless manifestation, into the ternary group distinguishable in *Buddhi* of which we have already spoken: the *Matsya Purāna* which we then quoted, declares that "in the Universal, *Mahat* (or *Buddhi*) is *Īshwara*"; and *Prājna* is also *Īshwara,* to Whom the *kārana-sharīra* properly belongs. It can also be said that the *Trimūrti* or " triple manifestation" is only the "outwardness" of *Īshwara*: in Himself the latter is independent of all manifestation, of which He is the principle, since He is Being itself; and everything that is said of *Īshwara,* as well in Himself as in relation to manifestation, can be said equally of *Prājna* which is identified with Him. Thus, apart from the special viewpoint of manifestation and of the various conditioned states which depend upon it within that manifestation, the intellect is not different from *Ātmā,* since the latter must be considered as "knowing itself by itself," form there is then no longer any reality which is really distinct from it, everything being comprised within its own possibilities; and it is in that "knowledge of the Self" the Beatitude strictly speaking resides.

"This one (*Prājna*) is the Lord (*Īshwara*) of all (*sarva,* a term which here implies, in its universal extension, the aggregate of the "three worlds," that is to say of all the states of manifestation comprised synthetically in their principle); He is omnipresent (since all is present to Him in integral knowledge and He knows directly all effects in the principial total cause, which is in no way distinct from Him);[10] He is the inward governor (*antaryāmī*, who, residing at the very centre of the being, regulates and controls all the faculties corresponding to the being's various states, while Himself remaining "actionless" in the fulness of His principial activity);[11] He is the source (*yoni*, matrix or primordial root, at the same time as principle or first cause) of all (that exists under any mode whatever); He is the origin (*prabhava*, by His expansion in the indefinite multitude of His possibilities) and the end (*apyaya*, by His return into the unity of Himself)[12] of the universality of beings (being Himself Universal Being)."[13]

References

1. Taoism likewise declares, "All is one; during sleep the undistracted soul is absorbed into this unity; in the waking state, being distracted, it distinguishes diverse beings" (*Chuang-tzu*, chap. II; French translation by Father Wieger, p. 215).
2. "To concentrate all one's intellectual energy as it were in one mass" is another expression of the Taoist doctrine bearing the same meaning (*Chuang-tzu*, chap. IV; Father Wieger's translation, p. 233). *Prajnāna* or integral Knowledge is here opposed to *vijnāna* or distinctive knowledge, which being specially applicable to the individual or formal realm, characterises the two preceding states; *vijnānamaya-kosha* is the first of the "envelopes" in which *Ātmā* is clothed on entering the "world of names and forms," that is to say when manifesting itself as *jīvātmā*.
3. *Māndūkya Upanishad*, shruti 5.
4. It is this which allows of the transposition in a metaphysical sense of the theological doctrine of the "resurrection of the dead," as well as the conception of "the glorious body"; the latter, moreover, is not a body in the proper sense of the word, but its "transformation" (or "transfiguration"), that is to say, its transposition outside form and the other conditions of individual existence; in other words it is the "realization" of the permanent and immutable possibility of which the body is but a transient expression in manifested mode.
5. The state of deep sleep has been described as "unconscious" by certain orientalists, who even seem tempted to identify it with the "Unconscious" of German philosophers like Hartmann; this error doubtless arises from the fact that they are unable to conceive of any consciousness other than individual and "psychological" consciousness; but their opinion appears none the less inexplicable, for it is not easy to see how, with such an interpretation, they are able to understand such terms as *Chit*, *Prajnāna* and *Prājna*.
6. The terms "subject" and "object," in the sense in which they are used here, cannot lead to any ambiguity: the subject is "the knower," the object is "the known" and their relation is knowledge itself. Nevertheless, in modern

philosophy, the sense of these terms and especially of their derivatives "subjective" and "objective" has varied to such a point that they have been given almost diametrically opposed interpretations, and some philosophers have taken them indiscriminately to indicate markedly conflicting meanings; besides their use often gives rise to considerable inconvenience from the point of view of clarity, and generally speaking it is advisable to avoid them as far as possible.

7. In Arabic we have, as equivalents of these three terms, intelligence (*el-Aqlu*), the Intelligent (*el-Āqil*) and the Intelligible (*el-Maqūl*): the first is universal Consciousness (*Chit*), the second is its subject (*Sat*) and the third is its object (*Ānanda*), the three being but one in Being " which knows Itself by Itself."
8. *Brihadāranyaka Upanishad,* Adhyāya IV, Brāhmaṇa 3, shruti 15; cp. *Brahma-sūtras,* Adhyāya I, Pāda 3, sūtra 8. See also our comments on the meaning of the word *nirvāna* which will appear in a later chapter.
9. It might be said, bearing in mind the reservations that we have made concerning the use of these words, that *Purusha* is the "subjective" pole of manifestation and *Prakriti* the "objective" pole; *Buddhi* then naturally corresponds to Knowledge, which is as it were a resultant of the subject and object, or their "common act," to use the language of Aristotle. However, it is important to note that in the order of Universal Existence it is *Prakriti* that "conceives" her productions under the "actionless" influence of *Purusha,* whereas in the order of individual existences, on the contrary, it is the subject that knows under the action of the object; the analogy is therefore inverted in this case as in those we have previously enumerated. Lastly, if intelligence be taken as inhering in the subject (although its "actuality" presupposes the presence of two complementary terms), one will be obliged to say that the universal Intellect is essentially active, while the individual intelligence is passive, at least relatively so (even though it be also active at the same time in another respect), and this is moreover implied by its "reflective" character, which again is fully in agreement with Aristotle's theories.
10. Effects subsist "eminently" in their cause, as has been said by the scholastic philosophers, and they are therefore constituents of its nature, since nothing can be found in the effects that was not to be found in the cause first of all; thus the first cause, knowing itself, knows all effects bye that very fact, that is to say it knows all things, in an absolutely direct and "non-distinctive" manner.
11. This "inward governor" is identical with the "Universal Ruler" referred to in the Taoist text quoted in an earlier note. The Far-Eastern tradition also says that "the Activity of Heaven is actionless"; according to its terminology, Heaven (*Tien*) corresponds to *Purusha* (considered at the various levels that we have already indicated) and Earth (*Ti*) to *Prakriti*; these terms are therefore not employed in the same sense that they must bear as constituent elements of the Hindu *Tribhuvana.*
12. In the cosmic order this can be applied to the two phases of "expiration" and "aspiration" occurring in respect of each cycle taken separately; but here it is the totality of cycles or states constituting universal manifestation that is referred to.
13. *Māndūkya Upanishad,* shruti 6.

Chapter 15

The Unconditioned State of Ātmā

"Waking, dreaming, deep sleep and that which is beyond, such are the four states of *Ātmā*: the greatest (*mahattara*) is the Fourth (*Turīya*). In the first three *Brahma* dwells with one of Its feet; It has three feet in the last."[1] Thus, the proportions previously established from one point of view are found reversed from another point of view: of the four feet (*pādas*) of *Ātmā*, the first three, when the states of *Ātmā* are considered distinctively, only have the importance of one from the metaphysical viewpoint, and from that same viewpoint the last is three in itself. If *Brahma* were not "without parts" (*akhanda*) it might be said that only a quarter of It is in Being (including therewith universal manifestation of which It is the principle) while Its three other quarters are outside Being.[2] These three other quarters may be regarded in the following manner: (1) the totality of the possibilities of manifestation insofar as they are not manifested, subsisting therefore in an absolutely permanent and unconditioned state, like everything belonging to the "Fourth" (insofar as they are manifested they belong to the first two states: as manifestable they belong to the third state, principial in relation to the two former); (2) the totality of the possibilities of non-manifestation (of which moreover we only speak in the plural by analogy, for they are evidently beyond multiplicity and even beyond unity); (3) lastly, the Supreme Principle of both, which is Universal Possibility, total, infinite and absolute.[3]

"The Sages think that the "Fourth" (*Chaturtha*),[4] which knows neither internal nor external objects (in a distinctive or analytical sense), nor the former and the latter taken together (regarded synthetically and in principle) and which is not (even) a synthetic whole of integral knowledge, being neither knowing nor not knowing, is invisible (*adrishta,* and indeed non-perceptible by any faculty at all), actionless (*avyavahārya,* in Its changeless identity), incomprehensible (*agrāhya,* since It comprehends all), indefinable (*alakshana,* since It is without any limit), unthinkable (*achintya,* since It cannot be clothed in any form), indescribable (*avyapadeshya,* since It cannot be qualified by any particular attribute or determination), the unique, fundamental essence (*pratyaya-sāra*) of the Self (*Ātmā,* present in all the states), without any trace of the development of manifestation (*prapancha-upashama,* and consequently absolutely and totally free from the special conditions of any mode of existence whatever), fulness of Peace and Beatitude, without duality: It is *Ātmā* (Itself, outside of and independently of any condition), (thus) It must be known."[5]

It will be noticed that everything concerning this unconditioned state of *Ātmā* is expressed under a negative form: it is easy to understand why this must be so, since, in language, every direct affirmation is necessarily particular and determinate, the affirmation of something which excludes something else, and which therefore limits the objects so affirmed.[6] Every determination is a limitation, that is to say, a negation:[7] consequently, it is the negation of a determination which is a true affirmation, and the apparently negative terms which we find there are, in their real sense, pre-eminently affirmative. So also the word "Infinite," which has a similar form, expresses in reality the negation of all limit; it is therefore the equivalent of total and absolute affirmation, which comprises or embraces all particular affirmations, but which is not any one affirmation to the exclusion of others, precisely because it implies them all equally and "non-distinctively": and it is in this manner that Universal Possibility contains absolutely all possibilities. Everything that can be expressed by means of an affirmative form belongs of necessity to the realm of Being, since this is itself the first affirmation or the first determination, that from which all others proceed, just as unity is the first of numbers whence all others are derived; but here we are no longer in unity but in "non-duality", or, in other words, we are beyond Being for the reason that we are beyond all determination, even principial.[8]

In Itself then *Ātmā* is neither manifested (*vyakta*) nor unmanifested (*avyakta*), so long at least as one only regards the unmanifested as the immediate principle of the manifested (which refers to the state of *Prājna*): but It is the principle both of the manifested and the unmanifested (although this Supreme Principle can also be said to be unmanifested in a higher sense, if only thereby to proclaim It absolute changelessness and the impossibility of characterizing It by any positive attribution whatsoever). "It (the Supreme *Brahma*, with which unconditioned *Ātmā* is identical), the eye does not attain to,[9] not speech, nor the mind:[10] we do not recognize It (as comprehensible by aught other than Itself) and it is for this reason that we do not know how to expound Its nature (by means of any sort of description). It is superior to what is known (distinctively, or superior to the manifested Universe) and It is even beyond what is not known (distinctively, or beyond the unmanifested Universe, one with pure Being);[11] such is the teaching that we have received from the wise men of former times. It should be realized that That which is not manifested by speech (nor by anything else), but by which speech is manifested (as well as everything else), is *Brahma* (in Its Infinity), and no what is looked upon (as an object of mediation) as "this" (an individual being or a manifested world, according as the point of view refers to the microcosm or the macrocosm) or "that" (*Īshwara* or Universal Being itself, outside all individualisation and all manifestation)."[12]

Shankarāchārya adds the following commentary to this passage: "A disciple who has attentively followed the exposition of the nature of *Brahma* must be led to suppose that he knows *Brahma* perfectly (at least in theory); but, in spite of his apparent justification for thinking so, this is nevertheless an erroneous opinion. In actual fact the well established meaning of every text concerning the Vedānta is that the Self of every being who possesses Knowledge is identical with *Brahma* (since through that very Knowledge the "Supreme Identity" is realized). Now a distinct and definite knowledge is possible in respect of everything capable of becoming an object of knowledge: but it is not possible in the case of That which cannot become such an object. That is *Brahma,* for It is the (total) Knower, and the Knower can know other things (encompassing them all within Its infinite comprehension, which is identical with Universal Possibility), but cannot make Itself the object of Its own knowledge (for, in Its identity, which is not the result of any identification, one cannot even make the principial distinction, as in the condition of *Prājna,* between a subject and an object which are nevertheless "the same," and It cannot cease to the Itself "all-knowing" in order to become "all-known," which would be another Itself), in the same way that fire can burn other things but cannot burn itself (its essential nature being indivisible just as, analogically, *Brahma* is "without duality").[13] Neither can it be said that *Brahma* is able to become an object of knowledge for anything other than Itself, since outside Itself there is nothing which can possess knowledge (all knowledge, even relative, being but a participation in absolute and supreme knowledge)."[14]

Hence it is said in the succeeding passage of the text: "If you think that you know (*Brahma*) well, what you know of Its nature is in reality but little; for this reason *Brahma* should be still more attentively considered by you. (The reply is as follows): I do not think that I know It; by that I mean to say that I do not know It well (distinctively, as I should know an object capable of being described or defined); nevertheless I know It (according to the instruction I have received concerning Its nature). Whoever among us understands the following words (in their true meaning): 'I do not know It, and yet I know It,' verily that man knows It. He who thinks that *Brahma* is not comprehended (by any faculty), by him *Brahma* is comprehended (for by the Knowledge of *Brahma* he has become really and effectively identical with *Brahma* Itself); but he who thinks that *Brahma* is comprehended (by some sensible or mental faculty) knows It not. *Brahma* (in Itself, in Its incommunicable essence) is unknown to those who know It (after the manner of some object of knowledge, be it a particular being or Universal Being) and It is known to those who do not know It at all (as "this" or "that")."[15]

REFERENCES

1. *Maitri Upanishad,* Prapāthaka 7, shruti 11.
2. *Pāda,* which means "foot" can also mean "quarter."
3. Similarly, when considering the first three states, which together constitute the realm of Being, it could also be said that the first two amount to no more than a third of Being, since they only contain formal manifestation, while the third state by itself amounts to two-thirds, since it includes both formless manifestation and unmanifested Being. It is essential to note that only possibilities of manifestation enter into the realm of Being, even when considered in all its universality.
4. The two words *Chaturtha* and *Turīya* bear the same meaning and apply to the one identical state: *Yad vai Chaturtham tat Turīyam* "assuredly that which is *Chaturtha,* that is *Turīya*" (*Brihadāranyaka Upanishad,* Adhyāya 5, Brāhmana 14, shruti 3).
5. *Māndūkya Upanishad,* shruti 7.
6. It is for the same reason that this state is simply called "the Fourth," since it

cannot be characterised in any way; but this explanation, although quite plain, has escaped the orientalists and in this connection one can mention a curious example of their lack of understanding: M. Oltramare imagined that this name "the Fourth" showed that a "logical construction" only was intended, because it reminded him of "the fourth dimension of the mathematicians"; this is an unexpected comparison to say the least, and it would certainly be difficult to justify it seriously.

7. Spinoza himself has formally recognized this truth: "*Omnis determinatio negatio est*"; but it is hardly necessary to mention that his application of it is more reminiscent of the indetermination of *Prakriti* than of that of *Ātmā* in its unconditioned state.
8. Our point of view in the present instance is purely metaphysical, but it should be added that the same considerations can also apply from the theological point of view; although the latter ordinarily keeps within the limits of Being, there are those who have recognised that "negative theology" alone is strictly valid, or in other words that only attributes which are negative in form can properly be ascribed to God. Cp. St. Dionysius the Areopagite, *Treatise on Mystical Theology*, the last two chapters of which resemble the text we have just quoted in a remarkable manner, even down to the expressions used.
9. Similarly the *Qurān* says in speaking of *Allah:* "The eye cannot reach Him." "The Principle is reached neither by sight nor by hearing." (*Chuang-tzu*, chap. XXII; Father Wieger's translation, p. 397.)
10. Here, the eye stands for the faculties of sensation and speech for the faculties of action; we have seen above that *manas*, by nature and function, participates in both alike. *Brahma* cannot be reached by any individual faculty: It cannot, like gross objects; be perceived by the senses, nor conceived by thought, like subtle objects; It cannot be expressed in sensible mode by words, nor in ideal mode through mental images.
11. Cp., the passage already quoted from the *Bhagavadgītā*, XV.18, according to which *Paramātmā* "transcends the destructible and even the indestructible"; the destructible is the manifested and the indestructible is the unmanifested, taken in the sense that we have just explained.
12. *Kena Upanishad*, Khanda I, shrutis 3-5. What has been said of speech (*vāch*) is then successively repeated, in shrutis 6-9, and in the selfsame terms, about the "mental faculty" (*manas*), the eye (*chakshus*), hearing (*shrotra*) and lastly about the "vital breath" (*prāna*).
13. Cp. *Brihadāranyaka Upanishad*, Adhyāya 4, Brāhmana 5, shruti 14: "How could the Knower (total) be known?"
14. Here again, one can establish a comparison with the following phrase from the *Treatise on Unity* (*Risālatul-Ahadīyah*) of Mohyiddin ibn Arabi: "There is nothing, absolutely nothing, that exists apart from Him (Allah), and he comprehends His own existence without (however) this comprehension existing in any manner whatsoever."
15. *Kena Upanishad*, Khanda II, shrutis 1-3. Here is an almost identical Taoist text: "The Infinite said: I do not know the Principle; this answer is profound. Inaction said: I know the Principle; this answer is superficial. The Infinite was right in saying that It knew nothing about the essence of the Principle. Inaction was able to say that it knew It as regards It external manifestations.... Not to know It is

to know It (in Its essence); to know It (in Its manifestations) is not to know It (as it really is). But how is one to understand this, that it is by not knowing It that It is known? This is the way, says the Primordial State. The Principle cannot be heard; that which is heard is not It. The Principle cannot be seen; that which is seen is not It. The Principle cannot be uttered; that which is uttered is not It.... The Principle, not being imaginable, cannot be described either. Whoever asks questions about the Principle and whoever answers them, both show that they do not know what the Principle is. Concerning the Principle, one can neither ask nor make answer what it is, (*Chuang-tzu,* chap. XXII; Father Wieger's translation, pp. 397-9).

Chapter 16

The Symbolical Representation of Ātmā and its Conditions by the Sacred Monosyllable Om

The rest of the *Māndūkya Upanishad* is concerned with the correspondence of the sacred monosyllable *Om* and its elements (*mātrās*) with *Ātmā* and its conditions (*pādas*): it explains on the one hand the symbolical reasons for this correspondence and, on the other hand, the effects of meditation bearing both on the symbol and on what it represents, that is to say on *Om* and on *Ātmā,* the former playing the part of "support" for attaining to knowledge of the latter. We will now give the translation of this final portion of the text; but it will not be possible to accompany it with a complete commentary, as that would carry us too far from the subject of the present study.

"This *Ātmā* is represented by the (supreme) syllable *Om,* which is represented in its turn by letters (*mātrās*), (in such a way that) the conditions (of *Ātmā*) are the *mātrās* (of *Om*), and (conversely) the *mātrās* (of *Om*) are the conditions (of *Ātmā*): these are *A, U* and *M.*

"*Vaishwānara,* whose seat is in the waking state, is (represented by) *A,* the first *mātrā,* because it is the connection (*āpti,* of all sounds, the primordial sound *A*, uttered by the organs of speech in their normal position, being as it were immanent in all the others, which are varied modifications of it and which are unified in it, just as *Vaishwānara* is present in all things in the sensible world and establishes their unity), and also because it is the beginning (*ādi,* both of the alphabet and of the monosyllable *Om,* as *Vaishwānara* is the first of the conditions of *Ātmā* and the basis starting from which metaphysical realization, for the human being, must be accomplished). He who knows this verily obtains (the realization of) all his desires (since, through his identification with *Vaishwānara,* all sensible objects become dependent upon him and form an integral part of his own being), and he becomes the first (in the realm of *Vaishwānara* or of *Virāj,* of which he makes himself the centre by virtue of that very knowledge and by the identification it implies when once it is fully effective).

"*Taijasa,* the seat of which is in the dream state, is (represented by) *U,* the second *mātrā,* because it is the elevation *(utkarsha,* of sound from its first modality, just as the subtle state is, in formal manifestation, of a more exalted order than the gross state) and also because it participates in both (*ubhaya,* that is to say, alike by its nature and by its position, it is intermediate between the two extreme elements of the monosyllable *Om,* just as the dream state is intermediate, *sandhyā,* between waking and deep sleep). He who knows this in truth advances along the path of Knowledge (by his identification with *Hiranyagarbha*), and (being thus illumined) he is in harmony (*samāna,* with all things, for he beholds the manifested Universe as the product of his own knowledge, which cannot be separated from him), and none of his descendants (in the sense of "spiritual posterity")[1] will be ignorant of *Brahma.*

"*Prājna,* the seat of which is in the state of deep sleep, is (represented by) *M,* the third *mātrā,* because it is the measure (*miti,* of the two other *mātrās,* as in a mathematical ratio the denominator is the measure of the numerator), as well as because it is the end (of the monosyllable *Om,* considered as containing the synthesis of all sounds, in the same way that the unmanifested contains, synthetically and in principle, the whole of the manifested with its diverse possible modes: the latter can indeed be considered as returning into the unmanifested, from which is was never distinguished save in a contingent and transitory manner; the first cause is at the same time the final cause, and the end is necessarily identical with the principle).[2] He who knows this is in truth the measure of this whole (that is to say the aggregate of the "three worlds" or of the different degrees of universal Existence, of which pure Being is the "determinant"),[3] and he becomes the final term (of all things, by concentration in his own Self or personality, where all the states of manifestation of his being are rediscovered, "transformed" into permanent possibilities).[4]

"The Fourth is "non-characterised" (*amātra,* unconditioned therefore): it is actionless (*avyavahārya*), without any trace of the development of manifestation (*prapancha-upashama*), abounding in Bliss and without duality (*Shiva Advaita*): that is *Omkāra* (the sacred monosyllable considered independently of its *mātrās*), that assuredly is *Ātmā* (in Itself, outside of and independently of any condition or determination whatever, even of the principial determination which is Being itself). He who knows this enters verily into his own "Self" by means of that same "Self" (without intermediary of any order whatsoever, without the use of any instrument such as a faculty of knowing, which can only attain to a state of the "Self" and not to *Paramātmā,* the supreme and absolute "Self")."[5]

As for the effects which are to be obtained by means of meditation (*upāsanā*) upon the monosyllable *Om,* in each of its three *mātrās* to begin with, and afterwards in itself and independently of its *mātrās,* we will only add that these effects correspond to the realization of different spiritual degrees, which may be described in the following manner: the first is the full development of the corporeal individuality; the second is the integral extension of the human individuality in its extra-corporeal modalities; the third is the attainment of the supra-individual states of being; finally, the fourth is the realization of the "Supreme Identity."

References

1. In this sense the expression has a more particular connection here with the "World-egg" and the cyclic laws, by reason of the identification with *Hiranyagarbha.*
2. In order to understand the symbolism we have just indicated, it must be borne in mind that the sounds *a* and *u* are combined in the sound *o,* and that the latter so to speak loses itself in the final nasal sound of *m,* without however being suppressed altogether, but on the contrary prolonging itself indefinitely, even while becoming indistinct and imperceptible. Furthermore, the geometrical figures that correspond respectively to the three *mātrās* are a straight line, a semicircle (or rather an element of a spiral) and a point; the first symbolises the complete unfolding of manifestation; the second, a state of envelopment relative to that unfolding, but nevertheless still developed or manifested; the third, the formless state devoid of "dimensions" or special limitative conditions, that is to say the unmanifested. It will also be noticed that the point is the primordial principle of all geometrical figures, representing in its own order the true and indivisible unity, in the same way that the unmanifested is the principle of all states of manifestation; this makes of the point a natural symbol of pure Being.
3. Were it not to involve too lengthy a digression, it would be possible to enter into a number of interesting considerations of a linguistic nature concerning the expression given to Being, conceived as the "ontological subject" and "universal determinant"; we will merely remark that in Hebrew the divine name *El* is related to this symbolism in particular. This aspect of Being is described in the Hindu tradition as *Swayambhū* "He who subsists by Himself"; in Christian theology it is

the Eternal Word considered as the *locus possibilium;* the Far-Eastern symbolism of the Dragon likewise refers to it.

4. It is only in this state of universalisation, and not in the individual state, that it can be said truly that "man is the measure of all things, of those things which are insofar as they are, and of those things which are not insofar as they are not," that is to say, metaphysically, of the manifested and the unmanifested; although, strictly speaking, one cannot speak of a "measure" of the unmanifested, if by "measure" is meant a determination by special conditions of existence, like those defining each state of manifestation. On the other hand, it goes without saying that the Greek sophist Protagoras, who is supposed to be the author of the formula we have just quoted (transposing the sense in order to apply it to "Universal Man"), was certainly very far from having attained to this conception; for in applying it to the individual human being, he only meant to express by it what the moderns would call a radical "relativism", whereas, for us, it implies something quite different, as will be readily understood by those who know the relationship existing between "Universal Man" and the Divine Word (cp. particularly St. Paul, *I Corinthians,* XV).
5. *Māndūkya Upanishad,* shrutis 8-12. Concerning the meditation on *Om* and its effects in various orders, relatively to the three worlds, further indications can be found in the *Prashna Upanishad,* Prashna V, shrutis 1-7. Also cp. *Chhāndogya Upanishad,* Prapāthaka I, Khandas 1, 4 and 5.

CHAPTER 17

The Posthumous Evolution of the Human Being

So far we have been considering the constitution of the human being, as also its different states, on the assumption that it subsists as a compound of the various elements that go to make up its nature, that is to say during the continuance of its individual life. It is necessary to emphasise the fact that the states which properly belong to the individual as such, that is to say not only the gross or corporeal state, as is obvious, but also the subtle state (provided of course that only the extra-corporeal modalities of the integral human state are included in it and not the other individual states of the being), are strictly and essentially states of the living man. This does not necessarily involve admitting that the subtle state comes to an end at the precise moment of bodily death and simply as a result thereof; on the contrary we shall see later on that a passage of the being into the subtle form takes places at that moment; but this passage is only a transitory phase in the reabsorption of the individual faculties from the manifested into the unmanifested, a phase the existence of which is quite naturally accounted for by the intermediate position occupied by the subtle state. It is however true that it may be necessary to envisage, in a particular sense and in certain cases at least, a prolongation and even an indefinite prolongation of the human individuality, which must needs be referred to the subtle, that is to say to the extra-corporeal modalities of that individuality; but such a prolongation is in no wise identical with the subtle state as it existed during earthly life. It must in fact be clearly understood that under the single heading of "subtle state" we are obliged to include extremely varied and complex modalities, even though we confine our viewpoint to the realm of purely human possibilities only; it is for this reason that we have taken care from the very beginning to point out that the term "subtle state" should always be understood relatively to the corporeal state, taken as a starting point and term of comparison; it thereby acquires a precise meaning solely by contrast to the latter state which, for its part, appears sufficiently well defined by the fact that it is the state in which we find ourselves at the present moment. Furthermore it will have been observed that among the five envelopes of the "Self" three are regarded as contributing to make up the subtle form (whereas one only corresponds to each of the other two conditioned states of *Ātmā*, in the one case because it really is only one particular and determinate modality of the individual, and in the other case because it is an essentially unified and "non-distinguished" state); and this is a further clear proof of the complexity of the state in which the Self uses this form as its vehicle, and this complexity must always be borne in mind if one is to follow the description of the different aspects from which it can be envisaged.

We have now to turn to the question of what is commonly called the "posthumous evolution" of the human being, that is to say to the consideration of the consequences for that being of death or—to explain more precisely what we mean by that term—of the dissolution of the compound which we have been discussing and which constitutes its actual individuality. It should be observed moreover that when this dissolution has taken place there is strictly speaking no longer any human being left, since it is essentially this compound which constitutes the individual man; the sole case where it is still possible to call the being in a certain sense human arises when, after bodily death, it remains in one of those prolongations of the individuality to which we have already alluded; in that case, although the individuality is no longer complete from the standpoint of manifestation (since the corporeal state is henceforth lacking, the possibilities corresponding to it having completed the whole cycle of their development), nevertheless certain of its psychic or subtle elements subsist without being dissociated. In all other cases the being cannot any longer be called human since it has passed out of the state to which that term applies and into another state, either individual or otherwise; thus the being which was formerly human has ceased to be so in order to become something else, in the same way that, through birth, it became human by passing from some other state into the state which we at present occupy. Besides, if birth and death be understood in their widest sense, that is to say as changes of state, it becomes at once apparent that they are modifications which correspond analogically to one another, being the beginning and the end of a cycle of individual existence; and indeed, if one were to place oneself outside the special viewpoint of a given state in order to observe the inter-connection of the different states with one another, it would be seen that they constitute strictly equivalent phenomena, death to one state being at the same time birth into another. In other words the same modification is either death or birth according to the state or cycle of existence in relation to which it is considered, since it marks the exact point common to both states or the transition from one to the other; and what is here true for different states is also true, on a different plane, for the various modalities of a given state, where those modalities are regarded as constituting, in the development of their respective possibilities, so many secondary cycles which are integrated in the totality of a more comprehensive cycle.[1] Finally, it is particularly important to add that "specification," according to the sense in which we have already used the expression (that is to say in the sense of attachment to a definite species such as the human species, which imposes certain general conditions upon a being, thus constituting its specific nature) is valid only within a given state and cannot be applied outside it. This must obviously be true, since the species is in no wise a transcendent principle in relation to this individual state, but pertains exclusively to the same domain, being itself subject to the limiting conditions which define that domain. For this reason the being who has passed into a different state is no longer human, since it no longer belongs in any way to the human species.[2]

The expression "posthumous evolution" calls for certain reservations, since it is only too liable to give rise to a number of ambiguities. In the first place, death being conceived as the dissolution of the human compound, the word "evolution" clearly cannot be understood here in the sense of the individual development, since we are concerned on the contrary with a reabsorption of the individuality into the unmanifested state;[3] this would amount rather to an "involution" from the particular point of view of the individual. Etymologically indeed these terms "evolution" and "involution" signify nothing more nor less than "development" and "envelopment";[4] but we are well aware that in modern language the word "evolution" has acquired quite a different meaning, which has almost converted it into a synonym for "progress." We have already had ample opportunities for expressing our views upon these quite recent ideals of "progress" and "evolution" which, by expanding themselves beyond all measure, have had the effect of completely corrupting the present-day Western mentality; it would be pointless to repeat ourselves here. We will merely recall that "progress" can only validly be spoken of in quite a relative sense, care always being taken to define in what respect it is used and within what limits; reduced to these proportions it no longer retains anything in common with that absolute "progress" which began to be spoken of towards the end of the eighteenth century and which our contemporaries are pleased to adorn with the name of "evolution," an expression that has a more "scientific" sound to their ears. Oriental thought, like ancient thought in the West, could not admit this notion of "progress," except in the relative sense that we have just given to it, that is to say as an idea of secondary importance, quite limited in scope and devoid of any metaphysical significance, since it belongs to that category of ideas which can only be applied to possibilities of a particular order and is not transposable outside certain limits. The "evolutionary" point of view does not admit of universalisation and it is not possible to conceive of the real being as something which "evolves" between two definite points or which "progresses," even indefinitely, in a fixed direction; such conceptions are devoid of meaning and show complete ignorance of the most elementary metapysical principles. At the most one might speak in a particular sense of the "evolution" of the being, in order to convey the idea of a passage to higher state; but even then it would be necessary to make a reservation preserving the full relativity of the term since, as concerns the being regarded in itself and in its totality, there can never be any question either of "evolution" or of "involution" in any sense whatever, its essential identity being in no wise altered by particular and contingent modifications of any sort, which can only affect one or other of its conditioned states.

A further reservation requires to be made with regard to the use of the word "posthumous": it is only from the particular point of view of human individuality and in so far as it is conditioned by time that one can speak of what is produced "after death" and likewise of what took place "before birth," so long at least as it is intended to preserve for the words "before" and "after" the chronological meaning which they normally convey. In themselves the states in question, if they exist outside the realm of human individuality, are in no wise temporal states and consequently cannot be situated chronologically; this is true moreover even of those states which include among their conditions some other mode of duration, that is to say of succession, once it is no longer temporal succession that is in question. As for the unmanifested state, it goes without saying that it lies outside all succession, so that the notions of anteriority and posteriority, even taken in the widest possible sense, cannot be applied to it in any way whatsoever. In this respect it may be remarked that, even during its lifetime, the being loses the notion of time when its consciousness has quitted the individual realm, as occurs in deep sleep and in ecstatic trance; so long as it remains in either of these states, which are truly unmanifested, time no longer exists for it.

Mention must still be made of the case where the posthumous state takes the form of a simple prolongation of the human individuality: this prolongation, it is true, may be situated in "perpetuity," that is to say in temporal indefinitude, or in other words in a mode of succession which still belongs to time (since we are not concerned with a state subject to conditions other that our own); but the time in question no longer has anything in common with the time in which bodily existence is carried on. Furthermore such a state is not among those which are of particular interest from the metaphysical point of view since, one the contrary, from that point of view it is the possibility of passing beyond individual conditions which must always be borne in mind rather than the possibility of remaining in them indefinitely; if we feel obliged, however, to refer to that state, it is chiefly for the sake of taking into account all possible cases and also because, as will be apparent later, this prolongation of human existence preserves for the being the possibility of obtaining "Deliverance" without passing through other individual states. Howbeit, leaving aside this last case, the following may be said: if non-human states are spoken of as situated "before birth" or "after death," this is primarily because they appear so in relation to human individuality; but it is also most important to realize that it is not the individuality which enters these states or which passes through them successively, since they are states which lie outside its sphere and which do not concern it as an individuality. Furthermore there is a sense in which the notions of anteriority and posteriority may be applied quite independently of the point of view of succession, temporal or otherwise; we are referring to that order, at the same time logical and ontological, in which the various states are interconnected and determine one another; thus if one state is the consequence of another, it may be said to be posterior to it. In such a manner of speaking use is being made of the temporal symbolism which serves to express the entire theory of cycles, although, metaphysically, it must always be remembered that there is perfect simultaneity between all the states, the point of view of actual succession being applicable only within a particular given state.

The foregoing remarks have been made with a view to forestalling any tendencies to attribute to the expression "posthumous evolution" (where it is thought advisable to use it in the absence of a more adequate term and in order to conform to certain habits of expression) an importance and a significance which it does not and could not really possess. We will now proceed to study those processes to which it relates, an understanding of which springs almost immediately from all the foregoing considerations. The exposition which follows is taken from the *Brahma-sūtras*[5] and from their traditional commentary (and by that we especially have in mind the commentary of Shankarāchārya), but we must point out that it is not a literal translation; here and there we shall find it necessary to summarise the commentary[6] and also to comment upon it in its turn, without which the summary would remain practically incomprehensible, as in fact very often happens where the interpretation of Oriental texts is concerned.[7]

References

1. These consideration relating to birth and death are moreover applicable to the point of view of the "macrocosm" as well as to that of the "microcosm"; though this is not the place to enlarge on this theme, readers may nevertheless gather some idea of how the implied consequences affect the theory of cosmic cycles.
2. It will be apparent that in the present context we are using the word "human" only in its precise and literal sense, applying solely to individual man; there is no question here of the analogical transposition that makes possible the conception of "Universal Man."
3. It cannot moreover be said that this entails a destruction of the individuality, because, in the unmanifested, the possibilities constituing it subsist in principle in a permanent manner, together with all the other possibilities of the being; nevertheless, since the individuality exists as such only in manifestation, it may

truly be said that on re-entering into the unmanifested it really disappears or ceases to exist *qua* individuality: it is not annihilated (for nothing that it can cease to be), but it is "transformed".

4. In this sense, but only in this sense, it would be possible to apply these terms to the two phases that are distinguishable in every cycle of manifestation, as we have already explained.
5. Adhyāya IV, Pādas 2, 3, and 4. The first Pāda of this fourth Adhyāya is devoted to the examination of the means of attaining Divine Knowledge, the fruits of which will be set forth in the following chapters.
6. Colebrooke has given a summary of this kind in his *Essays on the Philosophy of the Hindus* (Essay IV); but his interpretation, though it is not distorted by a systematic prejudice such as is only too frequent among other orientalists, is extremely defective from the standpoint of metaphysic, purely and simply through a lack of metaphysical insight.
7. It may be remarked, in this connection, that in Arabic the word *tarjumah* means both "translation" and "commentary", the one being looked upon as inseparable from the other; its nearest equivalent would therefore be "explanation" or "interpretation." It can even be said, where traditional texts are concerned, that a translation into a vernacular tongue, to be intelligible, should correspond exactly to a commentary written in the actual language of the text; a literal translation from an Oriental into a Western language is usually impossible and the more one strives to keep strictly to the letter, the greater the danger of losing the spirit; this is a truth which philologists unfortunately seem incapable of grasping.

Chapter 18

The Reabsorption of the Individual Faculties

"When a man is about to die, speech, followed by the remainder of the ten external faculties (the five faculties of action and the five faculties of sensation, manifested outwardly by means of the corresponding organs, but not identical with those organs themselves since they separate from them at this stage)[1] is reabsorbed into the inward sense (*manas*), the activity of the external organs coming to an end before that of this inward faculty (which is thus the final term of all the other individual faculties in question, just as it is their starting point and common source).[2] This latter faculty thereupon withdraws in the same way into the "vital breath" (*prāna*), accompanied in its turn by all the vital functions (the five *vāyus,* which are modalities of *prāna* and thus return into an undifferentiated state), these functions being inseparable from life itself; furthermore this same retreat of the inward sense is also to be observed in deep sleep and in ecstatic trance (accompanied by complete cessation of every external manifestation of consciousness)." We may add however that this cessation does not always necessarily imply total suspension of bodily sensibility, which constitutes a kind of organic consciousness, if one may describe it so; but under these circumstances the individual consciousness properly so-called will play not part in the manifestations of this sensibility, being no longer in communication with it as it normally is in the ordinary states of the living being; and the reason for this is easily understood, since, in point of fact, the individual consciousness no longer exists in the cases referred to, the real consciousness of the being having been transferred into a different state, which is really a supra-individual state. This organic consciousness to which we are alluding is not a consciousness in the true sense of the word, but it participates therein in some manner, owing its origin to the individual consciousness, of which it is a kind of reflection; separated from the latter it amounts to not more than a mere illusion of consciousness, but it can still present the appearance of consciousness to those who are only aware of externals,[3] in the same way that, after death, the persistence of certain more or less dissociated psychic elements, when they are able to manifest themselves, are able to present a similar and no less illusory appearance, as we have already explained in a different connection.[4]

"The 'vital breath', accompanied similarly by all the other functions and faculties (already reabsorbed into it and subsisting there as possibilities only, having now reverted to the state of indifferentiation whence they had to go forth in order to manifest themselves effectively during life) retires in its turn into the 'living soul' (*jīvātmā,* particular manifestation of the 'Self' at the centre of the human individuality, distinguishing itself from the 'Self' so long as that individuality endures as such, although this distinction is in fact purely illusory from the standpoint of absoulte reality, where there is nothing different from the 'Self'): and it is this 'living soul' which (as the reflection of the 'Self' and central principle of the individuality) governs the whole body of individual faculties (regarded in their integrality and not merely in their relationship with the bodily modality).[5] As a king's servants gather round him when he is about to go forth upon a journey, even so all the vital functions and faculties (external and internal) of the individual gather round the 'living soul' (or rather within it, out of which they all issue and into which they are all reabsorbed) at the final moment (of life in the ordinary sense of the word, that is to say of manifested existence in the gross state), when this 'living soul' is about to retire from its bodily form.[6] Accompanied thus by all its faculties (since it contains them and preserves them in itself as possibilities)[7] it withdraws, in an individual luminous essence (that is to say in the subtle form, which is compared to a fiery vehicle, as we saw when studying *Taijasa,* the second condition of *Ātmā*) composed of the five *tanmātras* or supra-sensible elementary essences (just as the bodily form is composed of the five *bhūtas* or corporeal and sensible elements), into a subtle state (in contrast to the gross state which is that of external or corporeal manifestation, of which the cycle is now completed so far as concerns the individual in question).

"Consequently (by reason of this passage into the subtle form, looked upon as luminous), the 'vital breath' is said to retire into the

Light, which does not mean to say the igneous principle exclusively (since we are really concerned with an individualized reflection of the intelligible Light, that is to say a reflection the nature of which is fundamentally the same as that of the mental faculty during corporeal life, and which moreover implies a combination of the essential principles of all five elements as its support or vehicle), nor does this withdrawal necessarily imply an immediate transition, since a traveller is said to go from one city to another even though he may pass successively through one or several intermediate cities.

"Furthermore this withdrawal or this abandonment of the bodily form (as described so far) is common alike to the ignorant person (*avidvān*) and to the contemplative Sage (*vidvān*) up to the point at which their respective (and henceforth different) paths branch; and immortality (*amrita,* but without immediate Union with the Supreme *Brahma* being thereupon attained) is the fruit of simple meditation (*upāsanā,* carried out during life without having been accompanied by any effective realization of the being's higher states), although the individual barriers resulting from ignorance (*avidyā*) may not yet be completely destroyed."[8]

An important comment is called for here as to the sense in which the immortality in question is to be understood: we have in fact pointed out elsewhere that the Sanskrit word *amrita* applies exclusively to a state which is beyond all change, whereas, by the corresponding word Westerners merely mean an extension of the possibilities of the human order, consisting in an indefinite prolongation of life (what the Far-Eastern tradition calls "longevity") under conditions which are to a certain degree transposed, but which always remain more or less similar to those of terrestrial existence, since they likewise concern the human individuality. Now in the present instance the state described is still an individual state and nevertheless it is said that immortality can be obtained therein; this may appear inconsistent with what we have just remarked, since it might be supposed that relative immortality only is meant, understood according to the Western sense: actually however that is not the case. It is indeed true that in order to be fully effective, immortality, in the metaphysical and Oriental sense, can only be obtained beyond all conditional states, individual or otherwise, in such a way that, being absolutely independent of any possible mode of succession, it is identical with Eternity itself; it would thus amount to an abuse of language to make this word apply to temporal "perpetuity" or to the indefinitude of any type of duration; but it is not in that sense that the expression is to be understood here. It must be realized that the idea of death is essentially synonymous with a change of state, which, as we have already remarked, is its widest acceptation; and when it is said that the being has virtually attained immortality, that is taken to mean that it will not need to pass through further conditioned states different from the human state, or to traverse other cycles of manifestation. This is not yet "Deliverance" actually realized, whereby immorality would be rendered effective, since the "individual barriers," that is to say the limitative conditions to which the being is subject, are not entirely destroyed; but it implies the possibility of obtaining that "Deliverance" directly from the human state, in the prolongation of which the being is maintained for the whole duration of the cycle to which that state belongs (which constitutes perpetuity properly so-called);[9] the being is thus enabled to take part in the final "transformation" which will be accomplished when the cycle is completed, causing everything that is then contained within it to return to the principial state of non-manifestation.[10] This is why the name "deferred Deliverance" or "Deliverance by degrees" (*krama-mukti*) is given to this possibility, since in this manner Deliverance is only obtained by means of intermediate stages (conditioned posthumous states) and not in a direct and immediate manner, as in other cases which we shall discuss later on.[11]

References

1. Speech is numbered the last when these faculties are considered in the order of their development; it must therefore be the first in the order of their reabsorption, since the order is now reversed.
2. *Chhāndogya Upanishad,* Prapāthaka VI, Khanda 8, shruti 6.
3. Just as, in a surgical operation, even the most complete anaesthesia does not always prevent the external symptoms of pain.
4. The organic consciousness we have just mentioned naturally enters into what the psychologists call the "subconscious"; but their chief error is to think that they have sufficiently explained a thing when all they have really done is to give it a name; besides, under that heading they have assembled the most heterogeneous collection of elements, without even being able to make a distinction between what is really conscious in some degree and what only appears to be so. Nor have they distinguished between the genuine "subconscious" and the "superconscious," in other words between factors assignable to states that are respectively higher and lower in relation to the human state.

5. It may be noticed that *prāna*, although it is outwardly manifested in respiration, is in reality distinct from the latter, since it would obviously be meaningless to say that respiration, a physiological function, separates from the organism and is reabsorbed in the "living soul." We will remind the reader once more that *prāna* and its various modalities belong essentially to the subtle state.
6. *Brihadāranyaka Upanishad*, Adhyāya IV, Brahmana 3, shruti 38.
7. A faculty is properly a power, that is to say a possibility, which is, in itself, quite independent of its actual exercise.
8. *Brahma-sūtras*, Adhyāya IV, Pāda 2, sūtras 1-7.
9. The Greek word α'ιωνιος really means "perpetual" and not "eternal," for it is derived from α'ιων (the same as the Latin *aevum*) which means an indefinite cycle; and this was also the original meaning of the Latin *saeculum* (French *siècle*) by which it is sometimes translated.
10. Much could be said on the subject of the translation of this final "transformation" into theological language in the Western religions, and especially about the conception of the "Last Judgement" which is closely bound up with it; but this would require extensive explanations and too complicated an exposition to be undertaken here, all the more so since, in practice, the characteristically religious point of view stops short at the consideration of a secondary cycle, beyond which a continuation of existence in the individual human state may still have to be taken into account; this would not be possible if the cycle to which that state belongs were being considered in its integrality. This must not be taken to mean, however, that the necessary transposition may not be effected from the religious point of view, as we have already explained when speaking of the "resurrection of the dead" and the "glorious body"; but, practically speaking, this transposition is not effected by those who cling to ordinary and "external" conceptions, and for whom nothing exists beyond human individuality; we will however, revert to this question when referring to the essential difference between the religious notion of "Salvation" and the metaphysical notion of "Deliverance."
11. It goes without saying that "deferred Deliverance" is the only kind that can be envisaged for the vast majority of human beings, which moreover does not mean that all will attain it indiscriminately, since it is also necessary to consider the case where a being, not having obtained even virtual immortality, must pass on into another individual state, in which it will of course enjoy the same possibility of attaining "Deliverance" as in the human state, but also, if one may so express it, the same possibility of not attaining it.

CHAPTER 19

Differences in the Posthumous Conditions according to the Degrees of Knowledge

"So long as it is in this condition (still individual, as has just been explained) the spirit (which, consequently, is still *jīvātmā*) of that person who has practised meditation (during his life, without attaining effective possession of the higher states of his being) remains attached to the subtle form (which may also be regarded as the formal prototype of the individuality, subtle manifestation representing an intermediate stage between the unmanifested and the gross manifestation and playing the part of immediate principle in relation to the latter); and it is associated, in this subtle form, with the vital faculties (in the state of reabsorption or principial contraction which has already been described)." It is admittedly necessary that there should still be a form in which the being can clothe itself, from the fact that its condition still belongs to the individual order; and this can only be the subtle form, since it has left the corporeal form and since moreover the subtle form must subsist after body, from having preceded it in the order of development in manifested mode, which is reproduced in inverse order in the return to the unmanifested; this does not however mean that this subtle form must in such a case be exactly the same as it was during bodily life, acting as the vehicle of the human being in the dream state.[1] We have already remarked that the individual condition itself, in an altogether general way and not merely as concerns the human state, can be defined as that condition in which the being is limited by a form; but it will be appreciated that this form is not necessarily determined as spatial and temporal, as is the case in the particular instance of the bodily state; it can in no wise be so in the non-human states, which are subject not be space and time, but to quite different conditions. As to the subtle form, if it does not altogether escape from time (although such time is not the same as that in which bodily existence is carried on) at least it escapes from space, and that is why one must on no account attempt to picture it as a kind of "double" of the body;[2] neither must it be looked upon as a "mould" for the body just because it is declared to be the formal prototype of the individuality at the origin of its manifestation;[3] we know only too well the Westerner's tendency to resort to the grossest representations and how many serious errors can arise in this way, so that we feel it imperative to offer every possible warning.

"The being may remain thus (in this same individual condition in which it is attached to the subtle form) until the outward dissolution (*pralaya,* the return into the undifferentiated state) of the manifested worlds (of the actual cycle, comprising both the gross and the subtle states, that is to say the whole domain of human individuality regarded in its integrality),[4] a dissolution in which it is plunged (together with the totality of beings in those worlds) into the bosom of the Supreme *Brahma*; but, even then, it may be united with *Brahma* only in the same way as in deep sleep (that is to say without full and effective realization of the 'Supreme Identity')." In other words and to use the language of certain Western esoteric schools, the case just referred to corresponds to a "reintegration in active mode," whereas genuine metaphysical realization is a "reintegration in active mode," the only mode which really implies a taking possession by the being of its absolute and final state. This is precisely what is meant by the comparison with deep sleep as it occurs in the life of the ordinary man; just as there is a return from that state to the individual condition, even so there can be a return to another cycle of manifestation for the being who is only united with *Brahma* in "passive mode," showing that the result obtained by the being while in the human state is not yet "Deliverance" or true immortality and that its case is in the final instance comparable (although with a notable difference as to the conditions of its new cycle) with that of the being who, instead of remaining until the *pralaya* in the prolongations of the human state, has passed after bodily death into another individual state. Besides this case, there is also the case where the realization of higher states and even of the "Supreme Identity," not having been obtained during life in the body, is achieved in the posthumous prolongations of the individuality; from being virtual, immortality then becomes effective, although this may not come about until the very end of the cycle: this is the "deferred Deliverance" of which we have already spoken. In both cases the being, which must be regarded as *jīvātmā* attached to the subtle form, finds itself for the whole duration of the cycle "incorporated"[5] so to speak in *Hiranyagarbha,* which is considered as *jīvaghana,* as we have already explained; it remains therefore subject to the special condition of existence which is life (*jīva*), by which the true sphere of *Hiranyagarbha* is delimited in the hierarchical order of Existence.

"This subtle form (in which the being, which thus remains in the human individual state, resides after death) is (in comparison with the bodily or gross form) imperceptible to the senses both as to its dimensions (that is to say because it is outside the spatial condition) and as to its consistency (or its particular substance, which is not made up of a combination of corporeal elements); consequently it does not affect the perception (or the external faculties) of those who are present when it separates from the body (after the 'living soul' has withdrawn into it). Neither is it affected by combustion or any other treatment which the body may undergo after death (which is the result of this separation, from the very fact of which no action of a sensible order can have any further repercussion on this subtle form, nor upon the individual consciousness which, remaining attached thereto, is no longer connected with the body). It is only sensible through its animating heat (its specific quality insofar as it is assimilated to the igneous principle)[6] so long as it inhabits the gross form, which becomes cold (and as a result inert as an organic whole) in death, as soon as it (the subtle form) has left it (although the other sensible qualities of the corporeal form still subsist without any apparent change), and which was warmed (and quickened) by it so long as it dwelt there (since it is precisely in the subtle form that the principle of individual life resides, so that it is only through the communication of its properties that the body can also be described as alive, by reason of the tie which exists between these two forms insofar as they are the expression of states of the same being, that is to say precisely up to the moment of death).

"But he who has obtained (before death, always understood as separation from the body) true knowledge of *Brahma* (implying effective possession of all the states of the being through metaphysical realization, apart from which there can only be an imperfect and purely symbolical knowledge) does not pass (in successive mode) through all the same stage of withdrawal (or of reabsorption of the individuality from the state of gross manifestation to the state of subtle manifestation, with the different modalities which this implies, and then to the unmanifested state, where individual conditions are at length entirely suppressed). He proceeds directly (into this latter state, and even beyond it, if it is only regarded as the principle of manifestation) into Union (already realized, at least virtually, during life in the body)[7] with the Supreme *Brahma,* with which he is identified (in an immediate manner), just as a river (here representing the current of existence through all states and all manifestations), at its mouth (which is the end or final term of that current) becomes identified (by intimate penetration) with the waves of the sea (*samudra,* the gathering together of the waters, symbolising the totalisation of possibilities in the Supreme Principle). His vital faculties and the elements of which his body is composed (all considered in principle and in their supra-sensible essence),[8] the sixteen component parts (*shodashā-kalāh*) of the human form (that is to say the five *tanmātras, manas* and the ten faculties of sensation and action), pass completely into the unmanifested state (*avyakta,* where, by transposition, they are all to be found in permanent mode, as changeless possibilities), this passage moreover implying no change for the being itself (of the kind implied in the intermediate stages, which necessarily include a variety of modifications, since they still belong to "becoming"). Name and Form (*nāma-rūpa,* namely the determination of the individual manifestation in its essence and its substance, as has been previously explained) also come to an end (as limiting conditions of the being), and, being "undivided," without the parts or members therefore which composed the earthly form (in the manifested state and insofar as that form was subject to quantity in its various modes),[9] he is set free from the conditions of individual existence (as well as from all other conditions applying to a special and determined state of existence of any sort, even a supra-individual state, since the being is henceforth in the absolutely unconditioned principial state)."[10]

Several commentators of the *Brahma-sūtras,* in order to bring out the nature of this "transformation" more vividly (we take the word in its strictly etymological sense, signifying "passage outside form"), compare it to the disappearance of water sprinkled upon a burning hot stone. This water is in fact "transformed" on contact with the stone, at least in the relative sense that it has lost its visible form (though not all form, since it clearly continues to belong to the corporeal order), without however its being possible to say on that account that it has been absorbed by the stone, since, actually, it has evaporated into the atmosphere, where it remains in a state imperceptible to sight.[11] Similarly, the being is in no wise "absorbed" on obtaining "Deliverance, although it may seem so from the point of view of manifestation, whence the "transformation" appears as a "destruction";[12] viewed from the standpoint of absolute reality, which alone remains for it, the being is on the contrary dilated beyond all limit, if one may use such an expression (which exactly translates the symbolism of steam from water spreading itself indefinitely through the atmosphere), since it has effectively realized the fulness of its possibilities.

References

1. There is certain continuity between the different states of the being, and all the more so between the various modalities which go to make up the same state of manifestation. The human individuality, even in its extra-corporeal modalities, must needs be affected by the disappearance of its bodily modality; moreover there are psychic, mental and other elements which have no reason for existing apart from their relation to bodily existence. Thus the disintegration of the body involves these other elements as well, for they continue to be associated with the body and are consequently also given up by the being at the moment of death, understood in the ordinary sense of the word.
2. Even the psychologists themselves recognize that the "mental faculty" or individual throught, the only kind they are able to understand, exists outside the spatial condition; it requires all the ignorance of a "neo-spiritualist" to wish to "localise" the extra-corporeal modalities of the individual and to suppose that the posthumous states are situated somewhere in space.
3. It is this subtle prototype, and not the bodily embryo, which in Sanskrit is referred to by the word *pinda,* as we mentioned before; this prototype moreover pre-exists individual birth, for it is contained in *Hiranyagarbha* from the beginning of the manifestation of the cycle, as representing one of the possibilities to be developed during the course of that manifestation; but its pre-existence is then only virtual, in the sense that it is not yet a state of the being of which it is destined to become the subtle form, since that being is not actually in the corresponding state, not yet existing, that is to say, as a human individual; and the same consideration applies by analogy to the bodily germ, if one regards it as also pre-existing in a certain sense in the ancestors of the individual in question, ever since the origin of mankind on this earth.
4. Universal manifestation viewed as a whole is often referred to in Sanskrit by the term *samsāra;* as we have explained before, it includes an indefinite series of

cycles, that is to say of states or degrees of existence, each of which terminates in *pralaya* like the cycle that more particularly concerns us here and really constitutes but one moment of the *samsāra*. Moreover we will repeat once again, to avoid any possible misunderstanding, that the interconnection of these cycles is really of a causal and not a successive order; in this respect all expressions drawn by analogy from the temporal order must be treated as purely symbolical.

5. This word, which we have used here to illustrate our meaning by means of the picture that it calls up, must not be taken literally, since the state in question has nothing corporeal about it.
6. As we have explained before, this animating warmth, represented as an inward fire, is sometimes identified with *Vaishwānara*, considered in this case no longer as the first of the conditions of *Ātmā* as previously described, but as the "Regent of Fire," as we shall see presently; *Vaishwānara* is then one of the names of *Agni*, and designates one of his functions and particular aspects.
7. If "Union" or the "Supreme Identity" has only been realized virtually, "Deliverance" takes place immediately at the very moment of death, but this Deliverance can also take place during life itself if "Union" has already been realized fully and effectively; the difference between these two case will be discussed in greater detail further on.
8. It may even happen, in exceptional cases, that the transposition of these elements is effected in such a way that the bodily form itself disappears without leaving any perceptible trace. Instead of being left behind by the being in the normal way, it passes over in its entirely either into the subtle or into the unmanifested state, so that properly speaking there is no death; in this connection, we have elsewhere recalled the Biblical examples of Enoch, Moses and Elijah,
9. The principal modes of quantity are expressly named in the following Biblical formula: "Thou hast disposed all things in weight, number and measure" (*Wisdom*, XI.21): the *Mene, Tekel, u-Pharsin* (counted, weighed, divided) of Belshazzar's vision (*Daniel*, V.25-28) corresponds word for word to this order (except that the first two terms are inverted).
10. *Prashna Upanishad*, Prashna VI, shruti 5; *Mundaka Upanishad*, Mundaka III, Khanda 2, shruti 8. *Brahma-sūtras*, Adhyāya IV, Pāda 2, sūtras 8-16.
11. Commentary of Ranganātha on the *Brahma-sūtras*.
12. That is why Shiva, according to the commonest interpretation, is looked upon as the "destroyer," whereas in reality he is the "transformer."

Chapter 20

The Coronal Artery and the "Solar Ray"

We must now return to the examination of what happens to the being who, not being "delivered" at the precise moment of death, has to pass through a series of degrees, represented symbolically as the stages of a journey and forming so many intermediate but not conclusive state which it is necessary to traverse before reaching the final goal. It should be remarked, moreover, that all these states, being still relative and conditioned, have no common measure with that state which alone is absolute and unconditioned; therefore no matter how exalted certain of them may be when compared with the bodily state, it would still seem that by obtaining them the being is no nearer to its final objective, which is "Deliverance"; and the whole of manifestation being strictly nil in comparison with the Infinite, it is evident that the difference between the states which go to make up manifestation must likewise be nil in Its presence, however considerable they may be in themselves; this holds good so long as the various conditioned states, which those differences separate one from another, are alone taken into account. However, it is none the less true that the passage to certain higher states constitutes as it were an advance towards "Deliverance;" but in that case it is gradual (*karma-mukti*), and may be compared to the use of certain appropriate means, such as those of *Hatha-yoga,* which are effective as a preparation, although there is certainly no possible comparison between these contingent means and the "Union" which it is intended to realize by using them as "supports."[1] But it must be clearly understood that "Deliverance," when realized, will always imply a discontinuity in relation to the state in which the being who obtains it finds himself and that, no matter what that state may be, this discontinuity will be of exactly the same order, since in all cases, between the state of the "undelivered" and that of the "delivered" being, there is no relationship such as exists between different conditioned states. The same is true even for states which are so far superior to the human state that, looked upon from the point of view of the latter, they might be taken for the goal towards which the being must ultimately tend; and this illusion is possible even with regard to states which are actually only modalities of the human state, although widely separated in every respect from the corporeal modality. It has seemed advisable to draw attention to this point in order to prevent any misunderstanding or erroneous interpretation, before continuing our exposition of the posthumous modifications which the human being can undergo.

"The 'living soul' (*jīvātmā*), with the vital faculties reabsorbed into it (and remaining there as possibilities, as has already been explained), having withdrawn into its own dwelling place (the centre of the individuality, described symbolically as the heart, as we saw at the beginning, wherein it dwells by reason of its being, in essence and independently of its conditions of manifestation, really identical with *Purusha,* from which it is separated only in an illusory manner), the apex (that is to say the most elevated portion) of this subtle organ (pictured as an eight-petalled lotus) shines[2] and illuminates the passage through which the soul must pass (to attain the various states about to be described), namely, the crown of the head, if the individual is a sage (*vidvān*), and another region of the organism (corresponding physiologically to the solar plexus)[3] if he is ignorant (*avidvān*).[4] A hundred and one arteries (*nādīs,* likewise subtle and luminous)[5] issue from the vital centre (as the spokes of a wheel issue from its hub), and one of these (subtle) arteries passes through the crown of the head (the region considered to correspond to the higher states of the being, insofar as their possibilities of communication with the human individual are concerned, as was seen in the description of the members of *Vaishwānara*); it is called *Sushumnā.*"[6] Besides this *nādī,* which occupies a central position, there are two others which play a particularly important part (notably as regards the correspondence in the subtle order with respiration, and consequently in the practices of *Hatha-yoga*): the one, situated on its right, is called *Pingalā*: the other, on its left, is called *Idā.* It is said furthermore that *Pingalā* corresponds to the sun and *Ida* to the moon; now we have seen above that the sun and the moon are described as the two eyes of *Vaishwānara*; these then are related respectively to the *nādīs* in question, while *Sushumnā,* being in the centre, is related to the "third eye", that is to say to the frontal eye of Shiva;[7] but we can only point out these connections in passing, since they lie outside our present subject.

"By this passage (*Sushumnā* and the crown of the head where it finishes), as a result of knowledge acquired and of consciousness of the meditated path (consciousness belonging essentially to an extra-temporal order, since, even when viewed in the human state, it is a reflection of higher states),[8] the soul of the sage, endowed (by virtue of the psychical regeneration which has made of him a man twice born, *dwija*)[9] with the spiritual grace (*prasāda*) of *Brahma,* which resides in this vital centre (relatively to the human individual concerned), escapes (frees itself of every link with the bodily condition which may still exist) and enters a solar ray (that is to say, symbolically, an emanation from the spiritual Sun, which is *Brahma* Itself, this time considered universally: this solar ray is nothing else than a particularisation, relatively to the being in question, or, if it be preferred, a 'polarisation' of the supra-individual principle *buddhi* or *mahat,* by which the multiple manifested states of the being are linked to one another and placed in communication with *Ātmā,* the transcendent Personality, which is identical with the spiritual Sun itself); it is along this route (described as the path of the 'solar ray') that it travels by night or by day, in winter or in summer.[10] The contact of a ray of the (spiritual) Sun with the *Sushumnā* is constant, so long as the body lasts (as a living organism and vehicle of the manifested being):[11] the rays of the (intelligible) Light, emitted from this Sun, reach this (subtle) artery, and, reciprocally (in reflected mode), extend from the artery to the Sun (as an indefinite prolongation by means of which communication, either virtual or effective, is established between the individuality and the Universal)."[12]

Everything that has just been said is completely independent of temporal circumstances and of all other similar contingencies which accompany death; that is not to say, however, that these circumstances are always devoid of any influence upon the posthumous condition of the being, but they have only to be considered in certain cases, which moreover we can but indicate here without further development. "The preference for summer, as an example of which the case of Bhīshma is cited, who waited for the return of this favourable season for his death, does not concern the sage who, in the contemplation of *Brahma,* has accomplished the rites (relative to 'incantation')[13] as prescribed by the Veda, and who has consequently acquired (at least virtually) the perfection of Divine Knowledge;[14] but it concerns those who have followed the observances taught by the Sānkhya or the Yoga-shāstra, in accordance with which the time of day and the season of the year are not matters of indifference, but have (for the liberation of the being leaving the bodily state after a preparation carried out in conformity with the methods referred to) an effective action as elements inherent in the rite (in which they intervene as conditions upon which the effects to be obtained depend)."[15] It goes without saying that, on the latter case, the restriction referred to only applies to beings which have stopped short at the attainment of degrees of realization corresponding to extensions of the human individuality; for one who has effectively transcended the limits of individuality, the nature of the means employed at the starting point of realization could have no influence of any kind on his subsequent condition.

References

1. An analogy might be drawn between what we have said here and what could likewise be said from the point of view of Catholic theology concerning the sacraments: in the latter also, the outward forms are properly-speaking "support", and these eminently contingent means produce a result which is of quite a different order from their own. It is by reason of his very nature and of the conditions governing it that the human individual requires such "supports" as a starting-point for a realization that extends far beyond them; and the disproportion between the means and the end corresponds to no more than the disproportion that exists between the individual state, taken as the basis for that realization, and the unconditioned state that is its term.

   We cannot develop here a general theory concerning the efficacy of rites; we will confine ourselves to saying by way of indicating the essential principle, that everything that is contingent insofar as it is a manifestation (except if it be a question of purely negative determinations) ceases to be so when viewed as a permanent and immutable possibility; everything that enjoys a positive existence must therefore be rediscovered in the Unmanifest, and it is this which allows of a transposition of the individual into the Universal, by the suppression of the limiting (therefore negative) conditions which are inherent in all manifestation.
2. Clearly this is another of those words which must be understood symbolically, since there is no question here of sensible fire, but rather of a modification of the intelligible Light.
3. The nerve plexuses, or, to be more exact, their counterparts in the subtle form (so long as the latter is linked to the bodily form) are symbolically described as "wheels" (*chakras*) or again as "lotuses" (*padmas* or *kamalas*). As for the crown of the head, it plays an important part also in the Moslem traditions concerning the posthumous conditions of the human being; and it would doubtless be possible

to find elsewhere practices depending on considerations of a similar order (the tonsure of Catholic priests for example), although in some cases the deeper reasons may have been forgotten.

4. *Brihadāranyaka Upanishad,* Adhyāya IV, Brāhmana 4, shrutis 1 and 2.
5. We would remind the reader that here we are not concerned with the bodily arteries of the blood stream, any more than with passages containing the air that we breathe; it is moreover quite obvious that, in the corporeal order, there cannot be any duct passing through the crown of the head, since no opening exists in that region of the organism. On the other hand, it should be observed that although the previous withdrawal of *jīvātmā* implies that the bodily form has already been abandoned, all relation between this and the subtle form has not yet been broken off in the phase we are now examining, since in describing the latter it is still possible to speak of the various subtle organs according to the correspondence which held good during physiological life.
6. *Katha Upanishad,* Adhyāya II, Vallī 6, shruti 16.
7. In the aspect of this symbolism which refers to the temporal condition, the Sun and the right eye correspond to the futures, the Moon and the left eye to the past; the frontal eye corresponds to the present which, from the point of view of the manifested, is but an imperceptible moment, comparable to the geometrical point without dimensions in the spatial order; that is why a single look from this third eye destroys all manifestation (which is expressed symbolically by saying that it reduces everything to ashes), and that is also why it is not represented by any bodily organ; but when one rises above this contingent point of view, the present is seen to contain all reality (just as the point carries within itself all the possibilities of space), and when succession is transmuted into simultaneity, all things abide in the "eternal present", so that the apparent destruction is truly a "transformation." This symbolism is identical with that of *Janus Bifrons* of the Romans, who had two faces, the one turned towards the past and the other towards the future, but whose real face, the one that gazes on the present, is neither of the two that can be seen.

   It should also be pointed out that the principle *nādīs,* by virtue of the same correspondence we have just mentioned, have a special connection with what might be called, in Western language, "human alchemy," wherein the organism is represented as the Hermetic *athanor;* this science, apart from the different terminology employed, closely resembles *Hatha-yoga.*
8. Therefore it is grave error to speak here of "remembrance" as Colebrooke has done in the essays we mentioned previously; memory, which is conditioned by time in the strictest sense of the word, is a faculty related to corporeal existence alone, and does not extend beyond the limits of this particular and restricted modality of human individuality; it is therefore numbered among those psychic elements we mentioned above, which are dissociated as a direct consequence of bodily death.
9. The conception of a "second birth", as we have already pointed out elsewhere, is one of those which are common to all traditional doctrines; in Christianity, in particular, psychic regeneration is very clearly represented by baptism. Cp. this passage from the Gospel: "Except a man be born again, he cannot see the Kingdom of God.... Verily, verily I say unto thee, except a man be born of water and of the Spirit, he cannot enter into the Kingdom of God.... Marvel not that

I said unto thee, ye must be born again." (*St. John*, III, 3-7). Water is looked upon by many traditions as the original medium of beings, by reason of its symbolism, as we explained earlier on according to which it stands for *Mūla Prakriti*; in a higher sense, by transposition, water is Universal Possibility itself; whoever is "born of water" becomes a "son of the Virgin" and therefore an adopted brother of Christ and His co-heir of the "Kingdom of God." On the other hand if one realizes that the "spirit" in the text just quoted is the Hebrew *Ruahh* (here associated with water as a complementary principle, as in the opening passage of *Genesis*) and if it be remembered the *Ruahh* also denotes air, we have the idea of purification by the elements, such as is to be met with in all initiatic as well as religious rites; and moreover, initiation itself is always looked upon as a "second birth," symbolically as long as it only amounts to a more or less external formality, but effectively when it is conferred in a genuine manner on one duly qualified to receive it.

10. *Chhāndogya Upanishad,* Prapāthaka 8, Khanda 6, shruti 5.
11. This, apart from any other consideration, should be sufficient to show that there is not question here of a ray of the Sun in the physical sense (for in that case uninterrupted contact would obviously be impossible) and that the reference can only be to the Sun in a symbolical sense. The ray which is connected with the coronal artery is also called *Sushumnā.*
12. *Chhāndogya Upanishad,* Prapāthaka 8, Khanda 6, shruti 5.
13. The word "incantation" as used here must be understood as referring essentially to an aspiration of the being towards the Universal with the object of obtaining an inward illumination, whatever may be the outward means, such as gestures (*mudrās*), words or musical sounds (*mantras*), symbolic figures (*yantras*) and so on, that can be employed as accessory supports of the inward act, and which have as their effect the production or rhythmic vibrations causing a repercussion throughout the indefinite series of states of the being. Such "incantation" has nothing whatever to do with the magical practices to which the same name is sometimes attached in the West, nor with a religious act such as prayer; all the methods in question are related exclusively to the realm of metaphysical realization.
14. We say virtually, because if this perfection were effective, "Deliverance" would by that very fact already have been obtained. Knowledge can be theoretically perfect, even though the corresponding realization has as yet only been partially accomplished.
15. *Brahma-sūtras,* Adhyāya IV, Pāda 2, sūtras 17-21.

CHAPTER 21

The "Divine Journey" of the Being on the Path of Liberation

The remainder of the symbolical journey to be carried out during the process of gradual liberation, starting from the end of the coronal artery (*Sushumnā*) and proceeding, in constant communication with a ray of the spiritual Sun, up to the final destination of the being, is effected by following the way marked by the path of this ray and retracing it (according to its reflected direction) back to its source, which is identical with that very destination itself. When we remember, however, that a description of this sort can apply to the posthumous states to be passed through successively both by those beings who obtain "Deliverance" on leaving the human state and also by those who, after the reabsorption of the human individuality, will be required on the contrary to pass into other states of individual manifestation, it will be evident that there must be two different itineraries corresponding to these two different cases; it is said, in fact, that the former follow the "Path of the Gods" (*devayāna*), whilst the latter follow the "Path of the ancestors" (*pitriyāna*). These two symbolical itineraries are summarized in the following passage from the *Bhagavadgītā*: "At what time those who tend towards Union (without having effectively realized it) quit manifested existence, either never to return or destined to return to it, I will teach thee, O Bhārata. Fire, light, day-time, waxing moon, the half year when the sun ascends towards the north, it is under these luminous signs that those go to *Brahma* who know *Brahma*. Smoke, night, waning moon, the half year when the sun descends towards the south, it is under these shadowy signs that there pass to the Sphere of the Moon (literally "attain the lunar light") those who later will return (to fresh states of manifestation). These are the two permanent paths of the manifested world (*jagat*), the one bright, the other dim; by the one they go to return no more (from the unmanifested to the manifested); by the other they go to return again (into manifestation)."[1]

The same symbolism is expounded in greater detail in various passages of the Veda. To deal with the *pitriyāna*, we will confine ourselves to remarking that it does not lead beyond the Sphere of the Moon; it follows that on that path the being is not set free from form, that is to say from the individual condition understood in its most general sense, since, as we have already remarked, it is precisely form which defines individuality as such.[2] According to certain parallels which we have pointed out before, this Sphere of the Moon represents the "cosmic memory";[3] it is on this account that it is the appointed abode of the *pitris*, that is to say of the beings belonging to the preceding cycle, who are regarded as the generators of the actual cycle, owing to that causal sequence of which the succession of cycles is but the symbol; this is the origin of the term *pitriyāna*, while *devayāna* naturally indicates the path leading to the higher states of the being, towards assimilation therefore with the very essence of the intelligible Light. It is in the Sphere of the Moon that forms which have completed the full course of their development are dissolved; and it is there also that are preserved the germs of forms as yet undeveloped, since in the case of form as of everything else, the starting point and the finishing point are necessarily to be found in the the same order of existence. For a further development of this subject it would be necessary to deal explicitly with the theory of cycle; here however it is sufficient to recall that each cycle being in reality a state of existence, the old form left off by a being not yet set free from individuality and the new form which it puts on necessarily belong to two different states (the passage from the one to the other taking place in the Sphere of the Moon, where the point common to both cycles is situated), since no being of any kind can pass through the same state twice, as we have explained elsewhere when pointing out the ineptitude of the "reincarnationist" theories invented by certain modern Westerners.[4]

We shall dwell at rather greater length upon the *devayāna* which is concerned with the effective identification of the centre of the individuality,[5] where all the faculties have previously been reabsorbed into the "living soul" (*jīvātmā*), with the very centre of the entire being, dwelling place of the Universal *Brahma*. We must again point out that the process in question only applies therefore in the case where that identification has not been realized during earthly life nor at the moment of death: once it has been achieved there is in fact no longer any "living soul" distinct from the Self, since the being is from that moment quit of the individual condition; that distinction, which never existed save in illusory mode (the illusion being inherent in the condition itself), ceases for being from the moment it attains absolute reality; the individuality disappears together with all limiting and contingent determinations, and the Personality alone remains in its fulness, containing all its possibilities in their permanent, unmanifested state principially within itself.

According to the Vedic symbolism, as found in various texts of the Upanishads,[6] the being which follows the *devayāna,* after having left the Earth (*Bhū,* that is to say the corporeal world or the sphere of gross manifestation), is first conducted to the light (*archis*), by which is meant here the Realm of Fire (*tejas*), the Ruler of which is *Agni,* also called *Vaishwānara* in a special signification of that name. It must be carefully noticed, moreover, that when we meet with the names of elements in the enumeration of these successive stages, this can only be in a symbolical sense, since all the *bhūtas* properly belong to the corporeal world, which is here represented in its entirety by the Earth (which, as element, is *Prithvī*); in reality then, the reference is to different modalities of the subtle state. From the Realm of Fire the being is led to the different kingdoms of the rulers (*devatās,* deities) or distributors of the day, of the bright half of the lunation (waxing period or first half of the lunar month),[7] of the six months when the sun is climbing northwards and finally of the year, all of which is to be taken a referring to the correspondences of these divisions of time (the "moments" of which the *Bhagavadgītā* speaks) analogically transposed into the extra-corporeal prolongations of the human state, and not as referring to these divisions themselves, which are literally applicable to the corporeal state only.[8] Thence it passes to the Realm of Air (*vāyu*), the Ruler of which (called by the same name) directs it towards the Sphere of the Sun (Sūrya or Āditya), and emerges from the upper limit of his kingdom through a passage likened to the nave of a chariot wheel, that is to say to a fixed axis around which the rotation or mutation of all contingent things takes place (it should not be forgotten that *vāyu* is essentially the "moving" principle), a mutation from which the being will henceforth escape.[9] It passes next into the Sphere of the Moon (Chandra or Soma), where however it does not remain like those following the *pitriyāna,* but whence it mounts to the region of the lightning (*vidyut*),[10] above which is the Realm of Water (*ap*), the Ruler of which is Varuna[11] (as, analogically, the lightning flashes beneath the rain-clouds). The reference here is to the higher or celestial waters, representing the totality of formless possibilities,[12] as opposed to the lower waters, which represent the totality of formal possibilities; there can be no further concern with the latter when once the being has transcended the Sphere of the Moon, since, as we remarked above, that is the cosmic region where the germs of the whole of formal manifestation are elaborated. Lastly, the remainder of the journey is carried out through the intermediate luminous region (*Antariksha,* which has been mentioned already, though with a somewhat different application, in the description of the seven members of *Vaishwānara*),[13] which is the Realm of Indra[14] occupied by Ether (*Ākāsha,* here representing the primordial state of undifferentiated equilibrium), up to the spiritual centre where *Prajāpati,* "Lord of produced beings," resides, who, as has already been pointed out, is the principial manifestation and direct expression of *Brahma* Itself in relation to the whole cycle or degree of existence to which the human state belongs. It is still necessary to take this state into account, although in principle only, since it is the one from which the being set forth; for even though it has been set free from form and individuality, it still retains certain ties with that state so long as it has not attained the absolutely unconditioned state, that is to say so long as "Deliverance" is not fully actualized for it.

In the various texts where the "divine journey" is described, certain variations are to be met with affecting the number and the order of enumeration of the intermediate stations, but they are of slight importance and more apparent than real; the foregoing exposition however is the result of a general comparison of these texts and can thus be regarded as a faithful expression of the traditional doctrine upon this question.[15] Besides, it is not our intention to embark upon a more detailed explanation of all this symbolism which will be, on the whole, clear enough as it stands to anyone who has some little familiarity with Oriental conceptions (we might even say with traditional conceptions in general) and their usual modes of expression; moreover its interpretation will be facilitated by all the illustrations we have already given, among which a considerable number of those analogical transpositions will have been met with, such as form the basis of all symbolism.[16] There is one point however which must be emphasised once again, even at the risk of repetition, because it is absolutely essential for the understanding of these matters. It must be clearly understood that when mention is made, for example, of the Spheres of the Sun and of the Moon, it is never the sun and the moon as visible stars, belonging purely to the corporeal realm, that are referred to, but rather the universal principles which these stars represent after their own fashion in the sensible world, including in certain cases the manifestations of these principles in different orders, in virtue of the analogical correspondences which interconnect all the states of the beings.[17] Indeed the different worlds (*lokas*), planetary Spheres and elementary Realms which are symbolically described as so many regions (only symbolically however, since the being who journeys through them is no longer subject to space), are in reality but different states.[18] This spatial symbolism (like the temporal symbolism which so often serves to express the theory of cycles) is natural enough and in sufficiently general use as to be unlikely to confuse any save those who are incapable of understanding anything but the most grossly literal meaning; such people will never realise the workings of a symbol, because their conceptions are irremediably limited to existence on this earth and to the corporeal world, within which, by the most naive of illusions, they wish to imprison the whole of reality.

The effective possession of these states can be obtained through identification with the principles which are described as their respective Rulers, and this identification operates in every case through knowledge, on condition that such knowledge is not merely theoretical; theory should only be looked upon as a preparation, which is however indispensable, for the corresponding realization. But, as regards each of these principles taken in itself and separately, the results of that identification do not extend beyond its particular domain, so that the obtaining of such states, which are still conditioned states, only constitutes a preliminary stage, a kind of approach (in the sense that we have already explained and with the restrictions which should be applied to such a manner of speaking) towards the "Supreme Identity," the ultimate goal attainable by the being in its complete and total universalisation; moreover the realization of this Identity, for those who have first of all to pass by the *devayāna*, may be deferred until the *pralaya*, as already stated, the transition from each stage to the next only becoming possible for the being who has obtained the corresponding degree of effective knowledge.[19]

Thus, in the case we are at present discussing, which is that of *krama-mukti*, the being may remain in the cosmic order until the *pralaya* without having attained effective possession of the transcendent states in which true metaphysical realization properly consists; but thenceforth, and from the very fact that he has passed beyond the Sphere of the Moon (that is to say emerged from the "current of forms"), he will none the less have obtained that "virtual immortality," which we defined previously. It is for this reason that the spiritual centre referred to above is still only the centre of a particular state or of a certain degree of existence, that to which the being, as a human being, belonged and to which it continues to belong in a certain manner, because its total universalisation in supra-individual mode is not actually accomplished; and this is also the reason for saying that in such a condition the bonds of individuality are not yet completely sundered. It is at this point precisely that conceptions which may properly be called religious stop short: as these conceptions always refer to extensions of the human individuality, the states to which they give access must necessarily preserve some connection with the manifested world, even when they reach beyond it; they are therefore not the same as those transcendent states to which there is no other means of access except pure metaphysical knowledge. This remark is especially applicable to the "mystical states"; and, as regards the posthumous states, there is precisely the same difference between "immortality" or "salvation," understood in the religious sense (the only sense normally taken into account in the West), and "Deliverance," as there is between mystical realization and metaphysical realization accomplished during earthly life. In the strictest sense, therefore, one can here only speak of "virtual immortality" and, as its final term, "reintegration in passive mode." Actually this last expression lies outside the religious viewpoint, as commonly understood, and yet it is through it alone that the relative sense in which religion uses the word "immortality" is justified and that a kind of link or transition can be established between it and the absolute and metaphysical sense in which the same term is understood by Orientals. All this moreover does not prevent us from admitting that religious conceptions are capable of a transposition by means of which they receive a higher and deeper meaning, for the reason that this meaning is also present in the sacred Scriptures upon which they are based; but by such a transposition they lose their specifically religious character, because this character is bound up with certain limitations, outside of which one has entered the purely metaphysical order. On the other hand a traditional doctrine such as the Hindu doctrine, which does not place itself at the point of view of the Western religions, does none the less recognise the existence of the states which are more particularly envisaged by those religions, and it must needs be so seeing that these states effectively constitute possibilities of the being; but such a doctrine cannot attribute to them an importance equal to that assigned to them by those doctrines which go no further (the perspective, if one may so put it, altering with the point of view) for going as it does beyond them, it is able to situate them in their exact place in the total hierarchy.

Thus, when it is said that the final goal of the "divine journey" is the World of *Brahma* (*Brahma-loka*), it is not the Supreme *Brahma* which is intended, not immediately at all events, but only its determination as Brahmā, who is *Brahma* "qualified" (*Saguna*) and, as such, considered as the "effect of the productive Will (*Shakti*) of the Supreme Principle" (*Kārya-Brahma*).[20] When Brahmā is mentioned in this case He must be regarded in the first place as identical with *Hiranyagarbha,* principle of subtle manifestation and thus of the whole domain of human existence in its integrality; and we have in fact previously remarked that the being which has attained "virtual immortality" finds itself so to speak "incorporated" by assimilation into *Hiranyagarbha;* and this state, in which it may remain until the end of the cycle (Brahmā existing as *Hiranyagarbha* for that cycle only), is what is most usually meant by the *Brahma-loka.*[21] However, just as the centre of each state of a being contains the possibility of identification with the centre of the total being, so the cosmic centre where *Hiranyagarbha* dwells is identified virtually with the centre of all the worlds:[22] that is to say that for the being who has passed beyond a certain degree of knowledge *Hiranyagarbha* appears as identical with a higher aspect of the "Non-Supreme"[23] which is *Īshwara* or Universal Being, first principle of the whole of manifestation. At this stage the being is no longer in the subtle state, not even in the purely principial sense, but is in the unmanifested; it retains a certain connection however the order of universal manifestation, of which *Īshwara* is properly the principle;

but it is no longer attached by any special links to the human state and to the particular cycle of which that state forms a part. This stage corresponds to the condition of *Prājna,* and it is the being who does not proceed beyond this condition who is described as united with *Brahma,* even at the time of the *pralaya,* in the manner of deep sleep only; the return thence to another cycle of manifestation is still possible; but, since the being is set free from individuality (as distinct from what occurs to one following the *pitriyāna*), that cycle can only be a formless and supra-individual state.[24] Finally, in the case where "Deliverance" is about to be obtained directly from the human state, still more is implied over and above what has just been described and in such a case the true goal is no longer Universal Being but the Supreme *Brahma* Itself, that is to say "unqualified" (*Nirguna*) *Brahma* in Its total Infinitude, comprising both Being (or the possibilities of manifestation) and Non-Being (or the possibilities of non-manifestation), principle of the one and of the other, beyond them both therefore,[25] while also at the same time containing them both, in accordance with the teaching that we have already expounded on the subject of the unconditioned state of *Ātmā,* which is precisely what is referred to in the present instance.[26] It is in this sense that the abode of *Brahma* (or of *Ātmā* in this unconditioned state) is even "beyond the spiritual Sun" (which is *Ātmā* in its third condition, identical with *Īshwara*),[27] just as it is beyond all the spheres of the particular states of existence, individual or supra-individual; but this abode cannot be directly attained by those who have only meditated upon *Brahma* through the medium of a symbol (*pratīka*), each meditation (*upāsanā*) only having in that case a definite and limited result.[28]

The "Supreme Identity," therefore, is the finality of the "liberated" being, that is, of the being who is freed from the conditions of individual human existence as well as from all other particular and limiting conditions (*upādhis*), which are looked upon as so many bonds.[29] When the man (or rather the being who was previously in the human state) is thus "delivered," the "Self" (*Ātmā*) is fully realized in its own "undivided" nature and is then, according to Audulomi, an omnipresent consciousness (having *chaitanya* as its attribute); the teaching of Jaimini is identical, but he specifies in addition that this consciousness manifests the divine attributes (*aishwarya*) as transcendent faculties, from the fact that it is united to the Supreme Essence.[30] Such is the nature of complete Liberation, obtained through the fulness of Divine Knowledge; as for those whose contemplation (*dhyāna*) has only been partial, although active (metaphysical realization remaining incomplete), or has been purely passive (as in the case of Western mystics), they enjoy certain higher states,[31] but without being able to arrive forthwith perfect Union (*yoga*), which is one and the same thing as "Deliverance."[32]

References

1. *Bhagavadgītā*, VIII, 23-26.
2. On the *pitriyāna*, see *Chhāndogya Upanishad*, Prapāthaka V, Khanda 10, shrutis 3-7; *Brihadāranyaka Upanishad*, Adhyāya VI, Brāhmana 2, shruti 16.
3. It is for this reason that it is sometimes said symbolically, even in the West, that everything that has been lost on this earth is recovered there (Cp. Ariosto, *Orlando Furioso*).
4. All that we have just said can also be related to the symbolism of *Janus;* the Lunar Sphere determines the separation of the higher (non-individual) states from the lower (individual) states; hence the double part played by the Moon as *Janua Coeli* (cp. the litanies of the Virgin in the Catholic liturgy) and *Janua Inferni,* a distinction corresponding to that between the *devayāna* and the *pitriyāna*. *Jana* or *Diana* is none other than the female form of *Janus;* and furthermore, *yāna* is derived from the same verbal root *i*, "to go" (Latin *ire*), which certain writers, Cicero in particular, also consider to contain the root of the name *Janus* itself.
5. It must be clearly borne in mind that this reference is to the integral individuality, and not to individuality reduced to its corporeal modality alone; moreover the latter no longer exists for the being in question, since it is the posthumous states that are under consideration here.
6. *Chhāndogya Upanishad*, Prapāthaka IV, Khanda 15, shrutis 5 and 6, also Prapāthaka V, Khanda 10, shrutis 1 and 2; *Kaushītaki Upanishad*, Adhyāya 1, shruti 3; *Brihadāranyaka Upanishad*, Adhyāya V, Brāhmana 10, shruti 1 and Adhyāya VI, Brāhmana 2, shruti 15.
7. This waxing period of lunation is called *pūrva-paksha* "the first part" and the waning period is called *uttara-paksha* "the last part" of the month. These expressions *pūrva-paksha* and *uttara-paksha* are also used in another connection with a totally different meaning: in an argument they refer respectively to an objection and to its refutation.
8. It would be interesting to establish the concordance of this symbolical description with similar descriptions given by other traditional doctrines (cp. for example the *Book of the Dead* of the Ancient Egyptians and the *Pistis Sophia* of the Alexandrian Gnostics); but this would take us too far afield. In the Hindu tradition, Ganesha, representing Knowledge, is at the same time known as the "Lord of deities"; his symbolism, in its relationship with the temporal divisions we have just been discussing, would give rise to developments of the greatest interest and also to most instructive comparisons with some ancient Western traditions; all these questions, which can find no place here, can perhaps be taken up again an another occasion.

9. To use the language of the Greek philosophers, we might say that it will have escaped from "generation" (γενεσις) and "corruption" (φθορα), terms that are synonymous with "birth" and "death" when these words are made to apply to all the states in individual manifestation; and from what has been said concerning the Lunar Sphere and its significance, one can also understand what those philosophers, and Aristotle in particular, meant when they taught that the sublunar world alone is subject to "generation" and "corruption"; this sublunar world, in fact, really represents the "current of forms" of the Far Eastern tradition; as for the Heavens, representing the formless states, they are necessarily incorruptible, that is to say there is no longer any dissolution or disintegration possible for the being which has attained to those states.
10. This word *vidyut* also comes from the root *vid,* by reason of the connection between light and sight; in its form it is very close to *vidyā*: the flash of lightning illumines the darkness; the latter is the symbol of ignorance (*avidyā*) while knowledge is an inner "illumination."
11. It may be noted, in passing, that this name is plainly the same as the Greek Ουρανος, although some philologists, for no very obvious reasons, have cast doubt on this identity; Heaven, called Ουρανος, is indeed clearly the same thing as the "Upper Waters" spoken of in *Genesis* which we meet with again here in the Hindu symbolism.
12. The *apsarās* are the celestial nymphs, which also symbolise these formless possibilities; they correspond to the *hūris* of the Moslem paradise; and this paradise (*Ridwān*) is the proper equivalent of the Hindu *Swarga.*
13. In that context we said that it is the medium in which forms are elaborated, because, in the scheme of the "three worlds," this region corresponds to the realm of subtle manifestation, stretching from Earth to the Heavens; here, on the contrary, the intermediate region in question is situated beyond the Lunar Sphere, therefore in the formless, and it is identified with *Swarga,* if one now understands by that word not the Heavens or higher states as a whole, but only their less elevated portion. It will again be noticed, in this connection, how a knowledge of certain hierarchical relationships makes it possible to apply one and the same symbolism at different levels.
14. *Indra,* whose name means "powerful", is also known as the Regent of *Swarga,* as can be explained by the identification indicated in the foregoing note; this *Swarga* is a higher state, but not a final one, and although formless, is still conditioned.
15. For this description of the various phases of the *devayāna,* see *Brahma-sūtras,* Adhyāya IV, Pāda 3, sūtras 1-6.
16. We will take this opportunity to apologise for having so multiplied the footnotes and for having allowed them to occupy more space than is usual; in dealing with interpretations of the kind here referred to, and also when establishing concordances with other doctrines, this method proved necessary in order to avoid breaking the thread of our exposition by too many digressions.
17. Natural phenomena in general, and especially astronomical phenomena, are never looked upon by the traditional doctrines otherwise than as a simple means of expression, whereby they symbolize certain truths of a higher order; and if they do in fact symbolize such truths, it is because their laws are fundamentally nothing but the expression of these very truths in a particular

domain, a sort of translation of the corresponding principles, naturally adapted to the special conditions of the corporeal and human state. It can therefore be seen how great is the error of those who imagine they have discovered "naturalism" in these doctrines, or who believe that the doctrines in question are only intended to describe and explain phenomena just as a "profane" science might do, though in a different form; this is really to reverse the true relationship, by taking the symbol itself for what it represents, the sign for the thing or the idea signified.

18. The Sanskrit word *loka* is identical with the Latin *locus*, "place"; it is worth noting that in the Catholic doctrine, Heaven, Purgatory and Hell are likewise described as "places," being in that case also taken symbolically to represent states, for there is never any question of these posthumous states being situated in space, even in the most external interpretation of this doctrine; such a misconception could only have arisen in the "neo-spiritualist" theories that have made their appearance in the modern West.
19. It is important to observe here that it is to the immediate realization of the "Supreme Identity" that the Brahmans have always attached themselves almost exclusively, whereas the Kshatriyas have for preference pursued the study of the states corresponding to the various stages of the *devayāna* as well as of the *pitriyāna*.
20. The word *kārya*, "effect," is derived from the verbal root *kri* "to make," with the addition of the suffix *ya* to mark an accomplishment in the future: "That which is to be made" (or to be still more exact "That which is going to be made," since *ya* is a modification of the root *i*, "to go"); this term therefore implies a certain notion of "becoming," which necessarily presupposes that whatever it applies to is only to be considered in reference to manifestation. Concerning the root *kri* we will point out that it is identical with that of the Latin *creare*, which proves that the latter word, in its original sense, simply meant "making"; the idea of creation as understood nowadays is of Jewish origin, and only attached itself to the word when the Latin language came to be employed for the expression of Judeo-Christian conceptions.
21. It is this which is the nearest equivalent of the "Heaven" or "Paradise" of the Western religions (in which, in this case, we may also include Islam); when a number of Heavens are considered (which are often represented by planetary correspondences), they should be understood as meaning all the states superior to the Lunar Sphere (which is itself sometimes looked on as the "first Heaven," under its aspect of *Janua Coeli*), up to and including the *Brahma-loka*.
22. Here again we are applying the fundamental analogy between the "microcosm" and the "macrocosm."
23. This identification of one aspect with another higher aspect and so on through different degrees up to the Supreme Principle, is after all, but the vanishing of so many "separative" illusions, which certain initiations represent as a series of veils that drop away in succession.
24. Symbolically, it is said that such a being has passed from the condition of a man to that of a *deva* (or what might be termed an "angelic" state in Western language); on the contrary, at the end of the *pitriyāna* there is a return to the "world of man" (*mānava-loka*), that is to say to an individual condition, so described by analogy with the human state, although it must of necessity be different, since

the being can never return to a state through which it has already passed.

25. We would however remind the reader that metaphysical Non-Being, like the Unmanifest (insofar as the latter is not merely identified with the immediate principle of manifestation, which is only Being), can be understood in a total sense whereby it is identified with the Supreme Principle. In any case however, a correlation between Non-Being and Being, or between the unmanifested and the manifested (even if in the latter case one goes no further than Being) can only be a purely apparent one, since metaphysically the disproportion that exists between the two terms does not permit of any real comparison between them.
26. In this connection, with the object of calling further attention to the agreement of the different traditions, we will once again quote a passage from the *Treatise on Unity* (*Risālatul-Ahadīyah*) of Mohyiddin ibn Arabia: "This immense thought (of the "Supreme identity") is only befitting to him whose soul is vaster than the two worlds (manifested and unmanifested). As for him whose soul is only as vast as the two worlds (namely one who attains Universal Being, but does not pass beyond it), it befits him not. For in truth this thought is greater than the sensible world (or the manifested world, for the word "sensible" must here to transposed analogically and not confined to its literal meaning) and the supra-sensible world (or the unmanifested, applying the same transposition) both taken together,"
27. On this point the orientalists, who have failed to grasp the real significance of the Sun through only taking it in its purely physical sense, have suggested some very strange interpretations; thus M. Oltramare writes rather naïvely: "By its risings and settings the sun consumes the life of morals; the liberated man exists beyond the world of the sun." Does this not convey the impression that it is merely a matter of escaping old age and attaining a corporeal immortality such as is sought by certain contemporary Western sects?
28. *Brahma-sūtras,* Adhyāya IV, Pāda 3, sūtras 7-16.
29. To these conditions words such as *bandha* and *pāsha,* the proper meaning of which is "bond", are applied; from the second of these two terms is derived the word *pashu,* which therefore means, etymologically, any living being bound by such conditions. Shiva is called Pashupati, "the Lord of beings in bondage," because it is by his "transforming" action that they are "delivered." The word *pashu* is often given a special meaning, to denote an animal victim in a sacrifice (*yajna, yāga* or *medha*), the victim being moreover "delivered" by the sacrifice itself, at least virtually so; but we cannot think of expounding here, even in summary fashion, a theory of sacrifice, which, taken in that sense, is essentially a means calculated to establish communication with higher states, and which is far removed from Western ideas of "redemption" or "expiation" and others of a like nature, ideas which are only intelligible from the specifically religious point of views.
30. Cp. *Brahma-sūtras,* Adhyāya, IV, Pāda 4, sūtras 5-7.
31. The possession of such states, which are identical with the various "Heavens", constitutes, for the being who enjoys it, a personal and permanent acquisition, notwithstanding their relativity (we are dealing always with conditioned, although supra-individual states); but the Western idea of "reward" must on no account be attached to this acquisition, for the simple reason that it is the fruit, not of

action but of Knowledge; moreover the notion of "reward," like that of "merit" of which it is the corollary, is an idea belonging exclusively to the moral order, which can find no place in the realm of metaphysic.

32. Knowledge, in this respect, is therefore of two kinds, and is itself described as "supreme" or "non-supreme" according to whether it concerns *Para Brahma* or *Apara Brahma* and leads therefore to the one or to the other.

CHAPTER 22

Final Deliverance

"Deliverance" (*moksha* or *mukti*), that is to say that final liberation of the being of which we have just spoken and which is the ultimate goal towards which the being tends, differs absolutely from all states which that being may have passed through in order to reach it, since it is the attainment of the supreme and unconditioned state, whereas all the other states, no matter how exalted, are still conditioned, that is to say subject to certain limitations which define them, making them to be what they are and characterizing them as determinate states. These remarks apply to the supra-individual states as well as to the individual states, in spite of the differences in their respective conditions; and even the degree of pure Being Itself, although it is beyond all existence in the strict sense of the word, namely beyond all manifestation both formless and formal, still implies a determination, which, though primordial and principial, is none the less already a limitation. It is through Being that all things in every mode of universal Existence subsist, and Being subsists through Itself; It determines all the states of which it is the principle and is only determined by Itself; but to determine oneself is none the less to be determined and therefore limited in some respect, so that Infinity cannot be attributed to Being, which must under no circumstances be regarded as the Supreme Principle. It is here that one may observe the metaphysical incompleteness of the Western doctrines, even of those, it must be admitted, in which some degree of true metaphysic is nevertheless present:[1] stopping short at Being, they remain incomplete even theoretically (without referring to realization, which they leave out of account altogether), and, as usually happens in such cases, they exhibit an undesirable tendency to deny that which lies outside their sphere and which, from the viewpoint of pure metaphysic, is precisely the most important part of all.

The acquisition or, to speak more accurately, the taking possession of higher states, whatever their nature, is thus only a partial, secondary and contingent result; and although this result may appear immense by comparison with the individual human state (and above all by comparison with the corporeal state, the only one effectually possessed by ordinary people during their earthly existence) it is none the less true that, in itself, it amounts strictly to nothing in relation to the supreme state, since the finite, while becoming indefinite through the extensions of which it is capable, that is to say through the development of its own possibilities, always remains nothing in comparison with the Infinite. Ultimately therefore a result of this kind is only of value by way of preparation for "Union," that is to say it is still only a means and not an end; to mistake it for the end is to continue in illusion, since all the states in question, up to and including Being, are themselves illusory in the sense we have attributed to that word from the beginning. Besides, in any state where some form of distinction remains, that is to say in all the degrees of Existence including those not belonging to the individual order, it is impossible for the universalisation of the being to become effective; and even union with Universal Being, according to the mode in which it is accomplished in the condition of *Prājna* (or in the posthumous state corresponding to that condition), is not "Union" in the full sense of the word; were it so, the return to a cycle of manifestation, even in the formless order, would no longer be possible. It is true that Being is beyond all distinction, since the first distinction is that of "essence" and "substance" or of *Purusha* and *Prakriti;* nevertheless *Brahma,* as *Īshwara* or Universal Being, is described as *savishesha,* that is to say as "implying distinction," since He is the immediate determining principle of distinction: only the unconditioned state of *Ātmā,* which is beyond being, is *prapancha-upashama,* "without any trace of the development of manifestation." Being is one, or rather it is metaphysical Unity itself; but Unity embraces multiplicity within itself, since it produces it by the mere extension of its possibilities; it is for this reason that even in Being Itself a multiplicity of aspects may be conceived, which constitute so many attributes or qualifications of It, although these aspects are not effectually distinguished in It, except insofar as we conceive them as such: yet at the same time they must be in some way distinguishable for us to be able so to conceive them. It might be said that every aspect is distinguishable from the others in a certain respect, although none of them in really distinguishable from Being, and that all are Being Itself;[2] we therefore find here a kind of principial distinction, which is not a distinction in the sense in which the word applies in the sphere of manifestation, but which is its analogical transposition. In manifestation distinction implies separation; but that separation has noting really positive about it, since it is only a mode of limitation;[3] pure Being, on the contrary, is beyond "separateness." Thus, that which exists at the level of pure Being is "non-distinguished, if distinction (*vishesha*) be taken in the sense applicable within the manifested states; and yet in another sense there is still present an element that is "distinguished" (*vishishta*): in Being all beings (meaning thereby their personalities) are "one" without being confused and distinct without being separated.[4] Beyond Being one cannot speak of distinction of any kind, even principial, although at the same time it cannot be said that there is confusion either; one is beyond multiplicity and beyond Unity as well; in the absolute transcendence of this supreme state none of these expressions can any longer be applied even by analogical transposition, and that is why recourse must be had to a term of negative form, namely to "non-duality" (*advaita*), as we have already explained; even the word Union in undoubtedly imperfect, because it evokes the idea of Unity, but we are obliged nevertheless to make use of it for the translation of the term *yoga,* since the Western languages have no alternative to offer.

Deliverance, together with the faculties and powers which it implies so to speak "by superaddition" (because) all states with all their possibilities are necessarily comprised in the absolute totalisation of the being), but which, we repeat, must only be considered as accessory and even "accidental" results and in no wise as constituting a final goal in themselves—Deliverance, we say, can be obtained by the *yogī* (or rather by him who becomes such in virtue of obtaining it), with the help of the observances indicated in the *Yoga-shāstra* of Patanjali. It can also be favoured by the practice of certain rites,[5] as well as of various particular styles of meditation (*hārda-vidyā* or *dahara-vidyā*);[6] but it must be understood that all such means are only preparatory and have nothing essential about them, for "man can acquire true Divine Knowledge even without observing the rites prescribed (for each of the different human categories, in conformity with their respective natures, and especially for the different *āshramas* or regular stages of life);[7] and indeed many examples are to be met with in the Veda of persons who have neglected to carry out such rites (the function of which is compared in the Veda to that of a saddle-horse, which helps a man to reach his destination more easily and more rapidly, but without which he is able to reach it all the same), or who have been prevented from doing so, and yet, by maintaining their attention perpetually concentrated and fixed on the Supreme *Brahma* (in which consists the one and only really indispensable preparation), have acquired true Knowledge concerning It (Knowledge which, for that reason, is likewise called "supreme").[8]

Deliverance, then, is only effective insofar as it essentially implies perfect Knowledge of *Brahma;* and, inversely, that Knowledge, to be perfect, presupposes of necessity the realization of what we have already termed the "Supreme Identity." Thus, Deliverance and total and absolute Knowledge are truly but one and the same thing; if it be said that Knowledge is the means of Deliverance, it must be added that in this case means and end are inseparable, for Knowledge, unlike action, carries its own fruit within itself;[9] and moreover within this sphere a distinction such as that of means and end can amount to no more than a mere figure of speech, unavoidable no doubt when one wishes to express these things, insofar as they are expressible, in human language. If therefore Deliverance is looked upon as a consequence of Knowledge, it must be specified that it is a strict and immediate consequence. This is most clearly affirmed by Shankarāchārya in the following terms: "There is no other means of obtaining complete and final Deliverance excepting Knowledge; it alone loosens the bonds of passion (and of all other contingencies to which the individual being is subjected); without Knowledge, Beatitude (*ānanda*) cannot be obtained. Action (*karma,* whether understood in its general sense or as applied specially to the performance of rites), not being opposed to ignorance (*avidyā*),[10] cannot remove it; but Knowledge disperses ignorance as light disperses darkness. As soon as the ignorance born of earthly affections (and other analogous bonds) is banished (and every illusion with it), the "Self" (*Ātmā*), by its own splendour, shines after (through every degree of existence) in an undivided state (penetrating all and illuminating the totality of the being), as the sun spreads its brightness abroad when the clouds have scattered."[11]

A most importance point to note is the following: action, no matter of what sort, cannot under any circumstances liberate from action; in other words it can only bear fruit within its own domain, which is that of human individuality. Thus it is not through action that it is possible to transcend individuality, taking individuality here moreover in its integral extension, for we do not for a moment pretend that the consequences of action are limited to the corporeal modality only; our previous remarks on the subject of life, which is in fact inseparable from action, will be found applicable in this instance. Hence it follows immediately that "Salvation" in the religious sense given to the world by Western people, being the fruit of certain actions,[12] cannot be identified with "Deliverance"; and it is all the more urgent to state this explicitly since orientalists constantly confuse the two together.[13] "Salvation" is properly speaking the attainment of the *Brahma-loka;* and we will further specify that by *Brahma-loka* must here be understood exclusively the abode of *Hiranyagarbha,* since any more exacted aspect of the "Non-supreme" lies outside individual possibilities. This accords perfectly with the Western conception of "immortality" which is simply an indefinite prolongation of individual life, transposed into the subtle order and extending to the *pralaya.* All this, as we have already explained, represents but one stage in the process of *krama-mukti;* moreover the possibility of a return into a state of manifestation (supra-individual however) is not definitely excluded for the being who has not passed beyond this stage. To go further and to free oneself entirely from the conditions of life and duration which are inherent in individuality, there is no other path but that of Knowledge, either "non-supreme" and leading to *Īshwara,*[14] or "supreme" and conferring immediate Deliverance. In the latter case there is no longer even occasion to consider a passage at death through various higher, though still transitory and conditioned states: "The Self (*Ātmā,* since there can be no further question of *jīvātmā,* all distinction and all 'separateness' having disappeared) of him who has attained the perfection of Divine Knowledge (*Brahma-vidyā*) and who has consequently obtained final Deliverance, ascends, on quitting its bodily form (and without passing through any intermediate stage), to the Supreme (spiritual) Light which is *Brahma,* and identifies itself with It, in an undivided and comfortable manner, just as pure water, mingling itself with the clear lake (without however losing itself in it in any way) conforms itself in every respect therewith."[15]

References

1. We are alluding only to the philosophical doctrines of antiquity and of the Middle Ages, since the points of view of modern philosophy are the very negation of metaphysic; and the above statement is as true of conceptions of a pseudo-metaphysical stamp as of those in which the negation is frankly expressed. Naturally, our present remarks only apply to doctrines that are known to the "profane" world, and do not refer to the esoteric traditions of the West, which, so long at least as they possessed a character that was genuinely and fully "initiatic," could not be limited in this way, but must on the contrary have been metaphysically complete under the twofold heading of theory and realization; these traditions however have never been known to any but an elect far more restricted in numbers than in the Eastern countries.
2. This can be applied, in Christian theology, to the conception of the Trinity: each Divine Person is God, but is not the other Persons. In scholastic philosophy the same might also be said of the "transcendentals," each one of which is co-extensive with Being.
3. In the individual states, separation is determined by the presence of form; in the non-individual states, it must be determined by some other condition, since these states are formless.
4. In this is to be found the chief difference separating the point of view of Ramanuja, who maintains the principial distinction, from that of Shankarāchārya, who transcends it.
5. These rites are in every respect comparable to those classed by the Moslems under the general denomination of *dhikr;* they are mostly based, as we have already mentioned, on the science of rhythm and its correspondences in all the various orders. Such are also the rites called *vrata* (vow) and *dwāra* (gate) in the otherwise partially heterodox doctrine of the Pāshupatas; under different forms all this is fundamentally the same as *Hatha-yoga* or at least equivalent to it.
6. *Chhāndogya Upanishad,* Prapāthaka VIII.
7. Furthermore, the man who has reached a certain degree of realization is called *ativarnāshramī,* that is to say beyond caste (*varna*) and beyond the stages of earthly existence (*āshramas*); none of the usual distinctions any longer apply to such a being from the moment that he has effectively transcended the limits of individuality, even though he has not yet arrived at the final goal.
8. *Brahma-sūtra,* Adhyāya III, Pāda 4, sūtras 36-38.
9. Besides, both action and its fruits are equally transient and "momentary"; whereas on the contrary Knowledge is permanent and final, and the same applies to its fruit which is not distinct from Knowledge itself.
10. Some would like to translate *avidyā* or *ajnāna* as "nescience" rather than "ignorance"; we confess that we cannot clearly see the need for this subtlety.
11. *Ātmā-bodha* (Knowledge of the Self).
12. The common expression "to work out one's salvation" is therefore perfectly accurate.
13. Thus M. Oltramare, for example, translates *moksha* by the word "Salvation" from beginning to end of his works, without seeming to suspect, we will not say the real difference which has been explained here, but even the mere possibility of inaccuracy in this identification.

14. It is hardly necessary to point out that theology, even if it comprised a realization rendering it truly effective, instead of remaining simply theoretical as is in practice the case (unless the "mystical states" can be said to represent such a realization, which is only partially and in certain respects true), would always be included in its entirety in this "non-supreme" Knowledge.
15. *Brahma-sūtras,* Adhyāya IV, Pāda 4, sūtras 1-4.

Chapter 23

Videha-mukti and Jīvana-mukti

Deliverance, in the case which has just been discussed, is properly speaking liberation achieved when "out of the bodily form (*videha-mukti*) and obtained in an immediate manner at the moment of death, Knowledge being already virtually perfect before the termination of earthly existence; it must be distinguished therefore from deferred and gradual liberation (*krama-mukti*), and it must also be distinguished from liberation obtained by the *yogī* during his actual lifetime (*jīvana-mukti*), by virtue of Knowledge no longer only virtual and theoretical but fully effective, that is to say by genuine realization of the "Supreme Identity." It must indeed be clearly understood that the body cannot constitute an obstacle to Deliverance any more than any other type of contingency; nothing can enter into opposition with absolute totality, in the presence of which all particular things are as if they were not. In relation to the supreme goal there is perfect equivalence between all the states of existence, so that no distinction any longer holds good between the living and the dead man (taking these expressions in the earthly sense). In this we note a further essential difference between Deliverance and "Salvation": the latter, as the Western religions conceive it, cannot be effectually obtained, nor even be assured (that is to say obtained virtually), before death; that which is attained through action can also always be lost through action; moreover there may be incompatibility between certain modalities of one particular individual state, at least accidentally and under particular conditions,[1] whereas there can no longer be anything of the kind once we are dealing with supra-individual states, and above all with the unconditioned state. To view things otherwise is to attribute to one special mode of manifestation an importance which it could not possess and which even manifestation in its entirety cannot claim; only the prodigious inadequacy of Western conceptions n regard to the constitution of the human being could render such an illusion possible, and only this could, moreover, give rise to any astonishment at the fact that Deliverance may be accomplished during life on earth as well as in any other state.

Deliverance of Union, which is one and the same thing, implies "by superaddition," as has already been said, the possession of every state, since it is the perfect realization (*sādhana*) and totalization of the being; besides, it matters little whether these states are actually manifested or not, since it is only as permanent and immutable possibilities that they have to be taken into account metaphysically. "Lord of many states by the simple effect of his will, the *yogī* occupies but one of them, leaving the others empty of life-giving breath (*prāna*), like so many unused instruments; he is able to animate more than one form in the same way that a single lamp is able to feed more than one wick."[2] "The *yogī*," says Aniruddha, "is in immediate contact with the primordial principle of the universe and in consequence (secondarily) with the whole of space, of time and of everything included therein," that is to say, with manifestation, and more particularly with the human state in all its modalities.[3]

Moreover it would be a mistake to suppose that liberation acquired when the being is quit of the bodily form (*videha-mukti*) is more complete than liberation "during life" (*jīvana-mukti*); if certain Westerners have made this mistake it is always as a result of the excessive importance they attach to the corporeal state, and what has just been said above dispenses us from further remarks on this subject. The *yogī* has nothing further to obtain subsequently, since he has actually realized "transformation" (that is to say a passing beyond form) within himself, if not outwardly; it matters little to him therefore that a certain formal appearance persists in the manifested world, since henceforth, for him, it cannot exist otherwise than in illusory mode. Strictly speaking it is only for other that the appearances persist thus without external change, and not for him, since they are now incapable of limiting or conditioning him; these appearances affect and concern him no more than does all the rest of universal manifestation. "The *yogī*, having crossed the sea of passions,[4] is united with Tranquillity[5] and possessed the Self (unconditioned *Ātmā*, with which he is identified) in its plenitude. Having renounced those pleasures which are born of perishable external objects (and which are themselves but external and accidental modifications of the being), and rejoicing in Bliss (*ānanda*, which is the sole permanent and imperishable object, and which is not different from the "Self"), he is calm and serene like the torch beneath an extinguisher,[6] in the fulness of his own essence (which is no longer distinguished from the Supreme *Brahma*). During his (apparent) residence in the body he is not affected by its properties any more than the firmament is affected by that which floats in its bosom (because, in reality, he contains all states within himself and is not contained by any one of them); knowing all things (and thereby being all things, not distinctively, but as absolute totality), he remains immutable, unaffected contingencies."[7]

Thus there is no spiritual degree superior to that of the *yogī* and it is evident that there cannot be; considered in his concentration within himself, he is also called *muni,* that is to say the "Solitary one,"[8] not in the popular and literal sense of the world, but as one who, in the fulness of his being, realizes the state of "perfect Solitude," which does not allow any distinction between outer and inner, nor any extra-principial diversity whatsoever to subsist in the Supreme Unity (or as we should say, to be strictly accurate, in "Non-Duality"). For him the illusion of "separateness" has finally ceased to exist, and with it every confusion engendered by the ignorance (*avidyā*) which produces and sustains that illusion,[9] for, "imagining first that he is the individual "living soul" (*jīvātmā*), man becomes afraid (through belief in the existence of some being other than himself), like one who mistakes[10] a piece of rope for a serpent; but his fear is dispelled by the certitude that he is not in reality this "living soul," but *Ātmā* Itself (in its unconditioned universality)."[11]

Shankarāchārya names three attributes correspond in a way to so many functions of the *sannyāsī,* the possessor of knowledge, who, if that Knowledge be fully effective, is none other than the *yogī:*[12] these three attributes are, in ascending order, *bālya, pānditya* and *mauna.*[13] The first of these words means literally a state comparable to that of a child (*bāla*):[14] it is a stage of "non-expansion," if one may so call it, where all the powers of the being are concentrated as it were in one point, realizing by their unification an undifferentiated simplicity, comparable to embryonic potentiality.[15] In a sense which is somewhat different, but which completes the foregoing (since it implies both reabsorption and plenitude), it also means the return to the "primordial state," of which all the traditions speak and which Taoism and Moslem esoterism stress more especially. This return is in fact a necessary stage on the path leading to Union, since it is only from this primordial state that it is possible to escape the limits of human individuality in order to rise to the higher states.[16]

A further stage is called *pānditya,* that is say "learning," an attribute indicating the teaching function; the possessor of Knowledge is qualified to communicate it to others or, more accurately speaking, to awaken corresponding possibilities within them, since Knowledge in itself is strictly personal and incommunicable. The *Pandita* therefore partakes more especially of the character of *guru* or "Spiritual Master";[17] but he may be in possession of the perfection of theoretical knowledge only, and for this reason it is necessary to take into account, as a still further and final stage, *mauna* or the state of *muni,* as being the only condition in which Union can genuinely be realized. There is yet another expression, *kaivalya,* which also means "isolation,"[18] and which at the same time expresses the ideas of perfection" and "totality"; this term is often employed as an equivalent of *moksha*: *kevala* denotes the absolute and unconditioned state which is that of the "delivered" being (*mukta*).

We have described the three attributes mentioned above as representing so many stages preparatory to Union; but obviously the *yogī* who has reached the supreme goal possesses each one of them *a fortiori,* since he possesses all states in the fulness of his essence.[19] These three attributes are implied moreover in what is called *aishwarya,* namely participation in the essence of *Īshwara,* for they correspond respectively to the three *Shaktis* of the *Trimūrti*: if it be understood that the fundamental characteristic of the "primordial state" is "Harmony," it will immediately be apparent that *bālya* corresponds to Lakshmī, while *pānditya* corresponds to Saraswatī and *mauna* to Pārvatī.[20] This point is of particular importance for understanding the nature of the "powers" which pertain to the *jīvana-mukta,* as secondary consequences of perfect metaphysical realization.

Furthermore the exact equivalent of the theory we have just mentioned is also to be found in the Far-Eastern tradition: this is the theory of the 'four Happinesses," the first two being "Longevity", which, as has already been remarked, is simply perpetuity of individual existence, and "Posterity," which consists in the indefinite prolongations of the individual through all his modalities. These two Happinesses therefore only concern the extension of the individuality and they are included in the restoration of the "primordial state", which implies their complete attainment; the remaining two, which refer on the contrary to the higher and extra-individual states of the being,[21] are the "Great Wisdom" and the "Perfect Solitude, that is to say *pānditya* and *mauna*. Finally these "four Happinesses" attain their fulness in a "fifth," which contains them all principially and unites them synthetically in their single and indivisible essence: no name is ascribed to this "fifth Happiness" (any more than to the "fourth state" of the *Māndūkya Upanishad*), since it is inexpressible and cannot be the object of any distinctive knowledge: it is however easy to see that we are concerned here with nothing less that Union itself or the "Supreme Identity," obtained in and through complete and total realization of what other traditions call "Universal Man," for the *yogī*, in the true sense of the word, like the "transcendent man" (*chenn-jen*) of Taoism, is also identical with "Universal Man."[22]

References

1. This restriction is indispensable, for if there were an absolute or essential incompatibility, the totalization of the being would thereby be rendered impossible, since no modality can remain unincluded in the final realization. Besides, the most exoteric interpretation of the "resurrection of the dead" is enough to show that, even from a theological viewpoint, there can be no irreducible antinomy between "salvation" and "incorporation."
2. Commentary of Bhavadeva Mishra on the *Brahma-sūtras*.
3. The following, a Taoist text, expresses the same ideas: "It (the being which has reached the state where it is united to the universal totality) will no longer be dependent on anything; it will be perfectly free.... It is also most justly said: the superhuman being has no longer an individuality of its own; the transcendent man has no longer any action of his own; the sage has not even a name of his own; for he is one with the All" (*Chuang-tzu*, chap. I: Father Wieger's translation, p. 211). The *yogī* or *jīvana-mukta*, is in fact liberated from both name and form (*nāma-rūpa*), which are the elements that constitute and characterise individuality; we have already mentioned the texts of the Upanishads where this shedding of name and form is expressly affirmed.
4. This is the region of the "Lower Waters" or formal possibilities; the passions are here taken as denoting the contingent modifications which go to make up the "stream of forms."
5. This is the "Great Peace" (*es-Sakīnah*) of the Moslem esoteric doctrine, or the *Pax Profunda* of the Rosicrucian tradition; the word *Shekīnah*, in Hebrew, denotes the "real presence" of the Divinity, or the "Light of Glory" in and by which, according to Christian theology, the "beatific vision" is brought about (cp. the "glory of God" in the already quoted text of the *Apocalypse*, XXI, 23). Here is another Taoist text referring to the same subject: "Peace in the void is an

indefinable state. It is neither taken nor given. One simply becomes established therein. Formerly one tended towards it. Nowadays the exercise of goodness and equity is preferred, which does not yield the same result." (*Lieh-tzu*, chap. I; French translation by Father Wieger, p. 77.) The "void" mentioned here is the "fourth state" of the *Māndūkya Upanishad*, which is in fact indefinable, being absolutely unconditioned so that it can only be spoken of in negative terms. The words "formerly" and "nowadays" refer to the different periods in the cycle of terrestrial humanity; the conditions of the present era (corresponding to the *Kali-yuga*) are such that the great majority of men become attached to action and feeling, which cannot lead them beyond the limits of their individuality, still less to the Supreme and unconditioned state.

6. This makes it possible to understand the real meaning of the word *nirvāna*, which Orientalists have misinterpreted in so many ways; this term, which is by no means peculiar to Buddhism as is commonly supposed, literally means "extinction of breath or of disturbance," the state therefore of a being which is not longer subject to any change or to any modification, nor to any of the other accidents or bonds of manifested existence. *Nirvāna* is the supra-individual condition (that of *Prājna*), while *parinirvāna* is the unconditioned state; the terms *nirvritti* "extinction of change or of action" and *parinirvritti* are also employed in the same sense. In the Moslem esoteric doctrine the corresponding terms are *fanā*, "extinction," and *fanā el-fanāi*, literally "extinction of the extinction."
7. Shankarāchārya's *Ātmā-bodha*.
8. The root of this word *muni* appears to be the same as that of the Greek μονος "alone", although some people have connected it with the term *manana*, which denotes reflective and concentrated thought; but this is most unlikely from the standpoint of etymological derivation, as well as from that of the meaning itself (for *manana*, derived from *manas*, can only properly apply to individual thought).
9. To this order, for instance, belongs "false imputation" (*adhyāsa*), which consists in ascribing to a thing attributes which do not really belong to it.
10. Such an error is called *vivarta;* it is properly speaking a modification which in no wise reaches the essence of the being to which it is attributed, and which therefore only affects the person who thus attributes it in consequence of an illusion.
11. Shankarāchārya's *Ātmā-bodha*.
12. The state of *sannyāsī* is strictly speaking the last of the four *āshramas* (the first three being the states of *Brahmachārī* or "student of the sacred Science," disciple of a *guru*, of *Grihastha* or "householder" and of *Vānaprastha* or "anchorite"); but the name *sannyāsī* is also sometimes extended, as in the present case, to the *sādhu*, that is to say to the man who has achieved perfect realization (*sādhana*) and who is *ativarnāshramī* as we have explained before.
13. Commentary on the *Brahma-sūtras*, Adhyāya III, Pāda 4, sūtras 47-50.
14. Cp. these words from the Gospels: "Suffer little children to come unto Me, for of such is the Kingdom of Heaven.... Whosoever shall not receive the Kingdom of God as a little child shall in no wise enter therein." (*St. Matthew*, XIX, 24; *St. Luke*, XVIII, 16 and 17.)
15. This state corresponds to the "concealed Dragon" of the Far Eastern symbolism. Another frequently used symbol is that of he tortoise which withdraws itself

entirely into its shell.

16. This is the "edenic state" of the Judaeo-Christian tradition; it explains why Dante placed the terrestrial Paradise on the summit of the mountain of Purgatory, that is to say at the exact point where the being quits the Earth, or the human state, in order to rise to the Heavens (described as the "Kingdom of God" in the foregoing Gospel quotation).
17. This is the *Sheikh* of the Moslem schools, also called *Murabbul-murīdīn;* the *Murīd* is the disciple, like the Hindu *brahmachārī.*
18. This again is the "void" referred to in the Taoist text quoted a little way back; and this "void" is also in reality the absolute fulness. [This use of the expression "the Void" (i.e., total absence of all particulars) as the equivalent of "the Infinite," is general in the Tibetan, and indeed in all Mahāyāna Buddhist doctrines. Full "realization" of the Void is therefore identical with the attainment of the ultimate goal of Liberation.—Translator]
19. It is also worth noticing that these three attributes, taken in the same order, are in a sense respectively "prefigured" by the first three *āshramas;* the fourth *āshrama,* that of the *sannyāsī* (to be understood here in its most usual sense), so to speak recapitulates and sums up the other three, just as the final state of the *yogī* embraces "eminently" all the particular states that have previously been traversed as so many preliminary stages.
20. Lakshmī is the *Shakti* of Vishnu; Saraswatī or Vāch is that of Brahmā; Pārvatī is that Shiva. Pārvatī is also called Durgā, that is to say "She who is difficult of approach." It is interesting to observe that something corresponding to these three *Shaktis* is to be found even in the Western traditions: thus, in Masonic symbolism the "three chief pillars of the Temple" are "Wisdom, Strength and Beauty"; here Wisdom is Saraswatī, Strength is Pārvatī and Beauty is Lakshmī. Similarly, Leibnitz, who had been the recipient of some esoteric teaching (rather elementary in character however) from a Rosicrucian source, describes the three principal divine attributes as being "Wisdom, Power and Goodness" which comes to exactly the same thing, for "Beauty" and "Goodness" are fundamentally but two aspects of a single idea, which is precisely the idea of "Harmony," as conceived by the Greeks and especially by Plato.
21. This explains how it is that the two first "Happinesses" fall within the province of Confucianism, whereas the two others pertain to the realm of Taoism.
22. This identity is similarly affirmed in the Moslem esoteric teaching concerning "the manifestation of the Prophet."

CHAPTER 24

The Spiritual State of the Yogī: The Supreme Identity

To give as exact an idea as possible of the state of the *yogī* who, through Knowledge, is "delivered in this life" (*jīvana-mukta*) and has realised the "Supreme Identity", we will once again quote Shankarāchārya[1]: his remarks on the subject, describing the highest possibilities to which the being can attain, may serve at the same time as a conclusion to the present study.

"The *yogī*, whose intellect is perfect, contemplates all things as abiding in himself (in his own Self, without any distinction of outer and inner) and thus, by the eye of Knowledge (*jnāna-chakshus*, a term which can be rendered fairly exactly by 'intellectual intuition'), he perceives (or rather conceives, not rationally and discursively, but by a direct awareness and immediate 'sensing') that everything is *Ātmā*.

"He knows that all contingent things (the forms and other modalities of manifestation) are not different from *Ātmā* (in their principle), and that apart from *Ātmā* there is nothing, 'things differing simply (in the words of the Veda) in attribution, accident and name, just as earthen vessels receive different names, although they are but different forms of earth';[2] and thus he perceives (or conceives, in the same as above) that he himself is all things (since there can no longer be anything which is "other" than himself or than his own 'Self').[3]

"When the accidents (formal and otherwise, including subtle manifestation as well as gross manifestation) are suppressed (these accidents only existing in illusory mode, in such a way that they are really nothing in relation to the Principle), the *muni* (taken here as synonym of the *yogī*) enters, with all beings (inasmuch as they are no longer distinct from himself) into the all-pervading Essence (which is *Ātmā*).[4]

"He is without (distinct) qualities and actionless;[5] imperishable (*askhara,* not subject to dissolution, which exercises dominion only over the manifold), without volition (applied to a definite act or to determined circumstances); abounding in Bliss, immutable, without form; eternally free and pure (unable to be constrained, reached or affected in any way whatsoever by anything other than himself, since this other is non-existent or at least experiences but an illusory existence, while he himself dwells in absolute reality).

"He is like Ether (*Ākāsha*), which is diffused everywhere (without differentiation) and which pervades the exterior and interior of things simultaneously;[6] he is incorruptible, imperishable; he is the same in all things (no modification affecting his identity), pure, impassible, invariable (in his essential immutability).

"He is (in the very words of the Veda) 'the Supreme *Brahma,* which is eternal, pure, free, single (in Its absolute perfection), continually abounding in Bliss, without duality (unconditioned) Principle of all existence, knowing (without that Knowledge implying any distinction of subject and object, which would be contrary to Its "non-duality") and without end'."

"He is *Brahma,* after the possession of which there remains nothing to possess; after the enjoyment of whose Bliss there remains no felicity to be desired; and after the attainment of the Knowledge of which there remains no knowledge to be obtained.

"He is *Brahma,* which once beheld (by the eye of Knowledge), no object is contemplated; being identified with which, no modification (such as birth or death) is experienced; which being perceived (but not however as an object perceptible by any kind of faculty), there is noting further to perceive (since all distinctive knowledge is thenceforth transcended and as it were annihilated).

"He is *Brahma,* which is disseminated everywhere and throughout all things (since there is nothing outside It and everything is necessarily contained in Its Infinity)[7]: in intermediate space, in that which is above and in that which is below (that is to say in the totality of the three worlds); the Real, abounding in Bliss, without duality, indivisible and central.

"He is *Brahma,* pronounced in the Vedānta to be absolutely distinct from that which It pervades (and which, on contrary, is not distinct from It or at Least only distinguishes itself from It in illusory mode)[8] continually abounding in Bliss and without duality.

"He is *Brahma,* 'by which (according to the Veda) are produced life (*jīva*), the inward sense (*manas*), the faculties of sensation and action (*jnānendriyas* and *karmendriyas*), and the elements (*tanmātras* and *bhūtas*) which compose the manifested world (in the subtle as well as in gross order)."

"He is *Brahma,* in which all things are united (beyond every distinction, even principial), upon which all actions depend (and which is Itself actionless); that is why It is disseminated throughout all things (without division, dispersion or differentiation of any sort).

"He is *Brahma,* which is without size or dimensions (unconditioned), without extension (being indivisible and without parts), without origin (being eternal), incorruptible, without shape, without (determined) qualities, without assignment or attribute of any kind.

"He is *Brahma,* by which all things are illuminated (participating in Its essence according to the degree of their reality), the Light of which causes the sun and all luminous bodies to shine, but which is not made manifest Itself by their light.[9]

"He himself pervades his own eternal essence (which is not different from the Supreme *Brahma*), and (simultaneously) he contemplates the whole World (manifested and unmanifested) as being (also) *Brahma,* just as fire intimately pervades a white-hot iron ball, and (at the same time) also reveals itself outwardly (by manifesting itself to the senses through its heat and its luminosity).

"*Brahma* resembles not the World,[10] and apart from *Brahma* there is naught (for, if there were anything apart from It, It could not be infinite); everything that appears to exist apart from It cannot exist (in this manner) save in illusory mode, like the apparition of water (mirage) in the desert (*maru*).[11]

"Of all that is seen, of all that is heard (and of all that is perceived or conceived by any faculty whatsoever) naught (veritably) exists apart from *Brahma;* and by Knowledge (principial and supreme), *Brahma* is contemplated as alone real, abounding in Bliss, without duality.

"The eye of Knowledge contemplates *Brahma* as It is in Itself, abounding in Bliss, pervading all things; but the eye of ignorance discovers It not, discerns It not, even as a blind man perceives not the sensible light.

"The 'Self' being illumined by meditation (when a theoretical and therefore still indirect knowledge makes it appear as if it were receiving the Light from a source other than itself, which is still an illusory distinction), and then burning with the fire of Knowledge (realising its essential identity with the Supreme Light), is delivered from all accidents (or contingent modifications), and shines in its own splendour, like gold which is purified in the fire.[12]

"When the Sun of spiritual Knowledge rises in the heavens of the heart (that is to say the centre of the being, called *Brahma-pura*), it dispels the darkness (of ignorance veiling the single absolute reality), it pervades all, envelopes all and illumines all.

"He who has made the pilgrimage of his own 'Self,' a pilgrimage not concerned with situation, place or time (or any particular circumstance or condition),[13] which is everywhere[14] (and always, in the immutability of the 'eternal present'), in which neither heat nor cold are experienced (no more than any other sensible or even mental impression), which procures a lasting felicity and a final deliverance from all disturbance (or all modification); such an one is actionless, he knoweth all things (in *Brahma*), and he attaineth Eternal Bliss."

REFERENCES

1. *Ātmā-bodha.* In grouping together a selection of passages from this treatise we shall not feel constrained to follow the order of the text too strictly; besides, in general, the logical sequence of ideas cannot be exactly the same in a Sanskrit text and in a translation into a Western language, by reason of the differences that exist between certain "ways of thinking" upon which we have laid stress on other occasions.
2. See *Chhāndogya Upanishad,* Prapāthaka VI, Khanda 1, shrutis 4-6.
3. It should be noted in this connection that Aristotle in his Περι Ψυχης, expressly declared that "the soul is all that it knows"; this sentence reveals a fair measure of agreement on this point between the Aristotelian and the Oriental doctrines, in spite of the reservations always called for on account of the difference between the respective points of view; but this affirmation, in the case of Aristotle and his successors, seems to have remained purely theoretical. It must therefore be admitted that the consequences of this idea of identification by Knowledge, as far as metaphysical realization is concerned, have continued quite unsuspected in the West, with the exception, as we have said before, of certain strictly initiatic schools, which had not point of contact with all that usually goes by the name of "philosophy."
4. "Above all things is the Principle, common to all, containing and penetrating all, of which Infinity is the proper attribute, the only one by which It can be characterised, for It bears no name of Its own." (*Chuang-tzu,* chap. XXV; translation by Father Wieger, p. 437.)
5. Cp. the "actionless activity" of the Far Eastern tradition.

6. Ubiquity is here taken as the symbol of omnipresence in the sense in which we have already employed this word above.
7. The reader may usefully be reminded here of the Taoist text we quoted earlier on at greater length: "Do not inquire whether the Principle is in this or in that; It is in all beings...." (*Chuang-tzu,* chap. XXII; Father Wieger's translation, p. 395.)
8. We would again call attention to the fact that this irreciprocity of relationship between *Brahma* and the World involves the formal condemnation of "pantheism," as well as of "immanentism" under all its forms.
9. It is "That by which all is manifested, but which is itself manifested by nothing", according to a text that we have already quoted (*Kena Upanishad,* Khanda I, shrutis 5-9).
10. The exclusion of any sort of pantheistic conception is here reiterated; faced with such clear statements, it is difficult to account for certain errors of interpretation which are so general in the West.
11. This word *maru,* derived from the root *mri,* "to die", applies to any barren region, entirely lacking in water, and more especially to a sandy desert, the uniform aspect of which can be taken as a support of meditation, in order to evoke the idea of the principial indifferentiation.
12. We have seen before that gold is looked upon as being itself of a luminous nature.
13. "Every distinction of place and time is illusory; the conception of all possible things (comprised synthetically in Universal Possibility, absolute and total) is effected without movement and outside time." (*Like-tzu,* chap. III; Father Wieger's translation, p. 107.)
14. Similarly in the Western esoteric traditions, it is said that the true Rosicrucians meet "in the Temple of the Holy Ghost, which is everywhere." It must be clearly understood that the Rosicrucians in question have nothing in common with the numerous modern organisations which have adopted the same name; it is said that shortly after the Thirty Years' War they left Europe and withdrew into Asia.

Index